Loan Collection

Lewis Kincheloe • Placa Rosa

Professional Photographers of America

Volume I 1998

Published by
MarathonPRESS *h*

Bienvenido a lo mejor de lo que puede ofrecer nuestra profesión. En las siguientes páginas encontrará las imágenes más significativas de miembros de Professional Photographers of America, los grandes contadores de la historia del mundo. Esta colección de préstamos, 1998 Loan Collection, es la recopilación de fotografías más importante del mundo. Entre los casi 8.000 trabajos presentados para nuestro concurso internacional se han seleccionado las aquí presentadas como „las mejores de las mejores". Dentro de poco disfrutará de un elenco de imágenes que va desde el retrato hasta las fotografías paisajísticas, desde restauraciones hasta reportajes de boda, desde componentes informáticas hasta comida preparada, realizadas tanto de forma tradicional como con la ayuda de las técnicas digitales.

En nombre de la Junta Directiva de los PPA quisiera expresar nuestro agradecimiento a todos aquellos que han trabajado duro para que se pudiera publicar este libro. Nuestro agradecimiento también va dirigido al comité de la exposición fotográfica, nuestro personal en PPA, los miembros del jurado internacional y los innumerables voluntarios que han trabajado durante largas horas para convertir esta publicación en una realidad. Y finalmente la más cordial bienvenida a nuestro miembro más reciente en el equipo: Marathon Press. Reconocido desde hace tiempo como líder en calidad en la impresión a cuatro colores, estamos felices de poder colaborar con ellos en esta publicación que representa la joya de la corona de PPA.

Así que tómese su tiempo y disfrute con las imágenes que verán a continuación; los fotógrafos representados en este libro seguro que marcan las diferencias en nuestra profesión.

Bert Behnke
M.Photog.Cr.Hon.M.Photog., reconocido por PPA
Presidente de los PPA 1997-1998

Bienvenue au meilleur de ce qu'offre notre profession! Les pages de ce livre présentent les plus belles images produites par les membres de l'organisme Professional Photographers of America, The World's Great Storytellers [les Grands Conteurs de ce Monde]. La Collection des Prêts 1998 est la première collection de photographies du monde. Sur les 8000 images ayant été présentées à notre concours international cette année, toutes celles qui ont été sélectionnées, ont été déclarées 'les meilleures des meilleures'. Vous êtes sur le point de découvrir une variété d'images qui couvre les thèmes allant du portrait, du paysage, de la restauration d'art, de l'album de mariage, des composants informatiques aux plats préparés, celles-ci étant réalisées tant traditionnellement qu'avec les dernières techniques numériques.

Au nom du Conseil d'Administration de PPA, je voudrais remercier tous ceux qui ont travaillé durement pour faire de ce livre une réalité. Sincères félicitations au comité des Expositions de Photographies, à l'ensemble du personnel de PPA, au jury international et à nos nombreux volontaires, qui ont offert de longues heures de travail afin de rendre possible cette publication. Pour finir, je voudrais souhaiter la bienvenue au plus récent membre de notre équipe, soit Marathon Press. Depuis longtemps reconnu comme leader dans le domaine de l'impression en quadrichromie, nous sommes très heureux de travailler avec eux sur cette réalisation, le joyau des publications de PPA.

Aussi, prenez le temps d'apprécier, d'étudier et de réfléchir aux images que vous êtes sur le point de voir, les photographes présentés dans ce livre faisant 'une réelle différence' dans la profession.

Bert Behnke
M. Photog. Cr., Hon. M. Photog., PPA Agréé
Président de PPA 1997-98

Willkommen zum Besten, was unser Beruf zu bieten hat. Auf den folgenden Seiten finden Sie die bedeutendsten Bilder von Mitgliedern der Professional Photographers of America, die großen Geschichtserzähler der Welt. Die 1998 Loan Collection ist die wichtigste Fotografiesammlung der Welt. Unter den fast 8000 Einsendungen zu unserem internationalen Wettbewerb wurden diese hier als „die Besten der Besten" ausgewählt. Sie werden gleich eine Palette an Bildern erleben, da von Portraits bis zu Landschaftsaufnahmen, von Restaurierungen bis zu Hochzeitsalben, von Computerkomponenten bis zu Speisen reicht, und die sowohl auf herkömmlich Art als auch mit Hilfe digitaler Techniken erstellt wurden.

Im Namen des Vorstandes der PPA möchte ich mich bei all denjenigen bedanken, die hart gearbeitete haben, damit dieses Buch veröffentlicht werden konnte. Unser Dank gilt dem Ausschuß der Fotografie-Ausstellung, unseren Mitarbeitern bei der PPA, den internationalen Preisrichtern und unzähligen Freiwilligen, die viele Stunden investiert haben, um diese Veröffentlichung möglich zu machen. Und letztendlich noch ein herzliches Willkommen für unser neuestes Team-Mitglied, Marathon Press. Seit langem als qualitativ führend auf dem Bereich des Vierfarb-Drucks anerkannt, schätzen wir uns sehr glücklich, mit ihnen bei dieser Veröffentlichung, der Kronjuwele der PPA, zusammenarbeiten zu können.

Nehmen Sie sich Zeit und genießen Sie die Bilder, die Sie gleich betrachten werden; die in diesem Buch vertretenen Fotografen machen sicher den Unterschied im Beruf deutlich.

Bert Behnke
M.Photog.Cr.Hon.M.Photog., anerkannt von der PPA
Vorsitzender der PPA 1997-1998

1998 Loan Collection Book （1998 年ローンコレクション・ブック）
PPA 会長の言葉

当界がお届けする最高級品へようこそ。本書は Professional Photographers of America （プロフェッショナル・フォトグラファーズ・オブ・アメリカ）の会員による最高の写真集、*the World's Great Storytellers* （ザ・ワールズ・グレイト・ストーリーテラーズ）です。1998 Loan Collection （1998 年ローンコレクション）は世界の写真の主要コレクションです。これらは、今年当方のインターナショナル・サロンコンペティションに参加した約 8 千近くの写真から、「最高中の最高」として選択されたものです。伝統的手法とデジタル技術の両者を駆使し、肖像から風景、修復物からウェディングアルバム、コンピュータコンポーネントから食品等全域にわたる写真が勢揃いしています。

PPA 理事会を代表し、本書の実現にご尽力いただいた皆様に感謝申し上げます。本書の出版を可能にするため多くの時間を捧げた Photographic Exhibitions committee （フォトグラフィック・エグジビションズ委員会）、PPA スタッフ、インターナショナル審査員、その他多数のボランティアの方々に賛辞を贈ります。最後に、最も新しいチームメンバー、高品質 4 色プリントのリーダーとしてかねてより名高い Marathon Press （マラソン・プレス）に歓迎の意を表します。皆様と共に PPA の珠玉である本書を出版できたことを大変嬉しく思います。

どうぞゆっくりお楽しみ下さい。目にされる写真をじっくりご覧になって、思いを巡らして下さい。本書で紹介するのは、まさに当界に「変革をもたらす」写真家達です。

Bert Behnke　（バート・ベーンク）
M. Photog. Cr., Hon. M Photog., PPA 認証
1997-98 年 PPA 会長

九八年美國專業攝影師珍藏集

會長的話

歡迎您欣賞這本收錄了我們行内最佳珍藏作品的攝影集！本集所展出的照片全是美國專業攝影師協會會員「以影象說故事」的傑作。「九八年美國專業攝影師珍藏集」是世界上第一本輯錄珍藏照片的攝影集，所有作品均從今年參加國際沙龍攝影比賽的接近八千幀照片選出，可說是超卓攝影作品的最優秀典範。翻閱這本珍藏集，從人物素描到山水風景，由翻新的古舊婚禮照片以至傳統電腦技術及最新數碼科技製作的美食影象，您將享受到全方位的視覺經驗。

我謹代表美國專業攝影師協會全體董事，向參與其事使珍藏集得以順利出版的人士致謝。本書的榮譽應該屬於照片展覽委員會、本會職員、國際評判，和無數日以繼夜工作不倦的義務工作人員。最後，我更要歡迎新加入成為我們成員之一，以優質四色印刷聞名的馬拉松印務。我們很高興能和他們合作，印製美國專業攝影師協會的瑰寶明珠「九八年美國專業攝影師珍藏集」。

這本珍藏影集代表的攝影名家絕非尋常之筆，請您細心欣賞，相信本書的影象能令您回味再三。

美國專業攝影師協會

白侯傑

九七至九八年度會長

PRESIDENT'S MESSAGE

Photo by Michael Taylor

Welcome to the best our profession has to offer. Presented on the following pages are the finest images produced by members of the Professional Photographers of America, the *World's Great Storytellers.* The 1998 Loan Collection is the premiere collection of photography in the world. Of the nearly 8000 images entered into our international salon competition this year, these were selected to be *"the best of the best".* You are about to experience an array of images that run the gamut, portraits to landscapes, restorations to wedding albums, computer components to prepared foods, done both traditionally and using digital techniques.

On behalf of PPA's board of directors I would like to thank all of those who work so hard to make this book a reality. Kudos to the Photographic Exhibitions committee, our PPA staff, the international jurors and countless volunteers who put in long hours to make this publication possible. And finally, welcome to our newest team member, Marathon Press. Long renowned as a leader in quality four-color printing, we are very happy to work with them on this, our crown jewel of PPA's publications.

So take the time to enjoy, study and reflect on the images you are about to view, the photographers represented in this book are truly *"Making a Difference"* in the profession.

Bert Behnke
M.Photog.Cr., Hon. M.Photog., PPA Certified
1997-98 PPA President

¡Bienvenidos al comienzo de una nueva tradición!

La presentación de las fotografías más significativas del concurso anual de PPA en un formato duradero e impreso ha sido uno de los objetivos de numerosos profesionales de la fotografía desde la aparición de los primeros trabajos en el libro ProPhotos 1 en el año 1978. Esta idea se retomó en el año 1990 publicando un segundo libro con las imágenes de este concurso, Proffesional Photographers Of America Loan Collection (Colección de préstamos de los fotógrafos profesionales de América). A lo largo de los años la idea de un libro con una cantidad reducida de imágenes ha ido creciendo para convertirse en una publicación anual y completa de toda la colección de préstamos.

En 1998 se tomaron varias medidas para lanzar el reinicio de estas publicaciones, enfocándolas hacia los progresos venideros de la fotografía profesional. Las fotografías calificadas como „préstamos" se publican en un libro bajo el título PPA Loan Collection (Colección de préstamos de los PPA). Otro libro, totalmente nuevo,- PPA Showcase (Vitrina PPA) - contiene una selección de imágenes de la colección general PPA General Collection. Ambas publicaciones se presentan con un nuevo diseño y bajo nuevos nombres para que el reconocimiento visual resulta más fácil al igual que facilite una mejor conexión con la identidad de los PPA Stroyteller (contadores de la historia).

PPA Showcase además acentúa el valor formativo de estas publicaciones. Y, aunque ambas publicaciones sean complementarias entre ellas ¡cada uno de los libros por sí solo ya es único! La PPA Loan Collection mantiene su formato y tamaño tradicional, mientras que PPA Showcase no sólo se publica en un formato único y novedoso, sino que contiene además en cada página una imagen individual de un fotógrafo.

Nuestra más sinceras felicitaciones no van dirigidas únicamente a los fotógrafos cuya creatividad queda representada en estas publicaciones, sino también a todos aquellos profesionales, que se han tomado el tiempo y las molestias para participar en el International Judging & Annual Exhibition of Professional Photography (Concurso internacional y exhibición anual de fotografía profesional) de PPA.

Como sabe todo el que en alguna ocasión ha participado en un concurso artístico, no resulta fácil - ni cómodo - desnudar su creatividad ante la crítica, pero a la larga esto puede ser enriquecedor y provechoso.

Rex Alewel, *Editor*

Vive le renouveau d'une tradition qui dure!

Présenter les images étonnantes du concours annuel du PPA dans un format de qualité et qui dure, a toujours été un but pour nos professionnels de la photographie, et ce dès 1978, date à laquelle nous avons publié ProPhoto 1. Nous avons renouvelé cette idée en 1990 avec la publication d'un second numéro présentant les images de ce même concours, sous le titre Professional Photographers of America Loan Collection.Aujourd'hui, nous sommes passés d'un livre contenant un nombre limités d'images à une publication annuelle présentant l'entière collection.

En 1998, nous avons franchi plusieurs étapes afin de donner un aspect de renouveau à ces publications, qui incluent les derniers progrès de création et de fabrication d'images professionnelles. Les images récompensées du statut de «prêt » ('loan') sont maintenant publiées dans le livre PPA Loan Collection. Un second livre, entièrement nouveau – PPA Showcase – contient une sélection des images de la Collection Générale du PPA. Chacune de ces publications a été recréée et reformulée, afin de renforcer leur originalité visuelle et leur lien direct avec l'esprit des Conteurs du PPA ['PPA Storytellers'].

La parution du livre PPA Showcase étend la valeur éducative de nos publications. De plus, bien que ces deux publications annuelles se complètent, elles restent profondément uniques! Si le livre PPA Loan Collection garde ses taille et forme traditionnelles, le livre PPA Showcase au format nouveau et original offre quant à lui, sur chacune de ses pages, une seule image d'un photographe.

Toutes nos sincères félicitations ne s'adressent pas uniquement à tous les photographes dont la créativité est présentée dans nos publications, mais aussi à toutes celles et tous ceux qui rendent ces images possibles, et qui ont pris le temps de participer au Concours International et Exposition Annuelle de la Photographie Professionnelle du PPA. Tous ceux qui ont déjà participé à un concours artistique savent que ce n'est pas toujours facile et agréable d'offrir à la critique sa créativité, même si à long terme, cet effort rapporte à l'artiste enrichissement et reconnaissance.

Recevez mes sincères compliments,
Rex Alewel, *Editeur*

Willkommen zum Anfang einer neuen Tradition!

Die Veröffentlichung der bedeutendsten Bilder des jährlichen PPA-Wettbewerbs in einem beständigen, ausgedruckten Format war ein Ziel zahlreicher Fotoprofis, seit der Ausgabe der ersten Arbeiten in ProPhotos 1 im Jahr 1978. Die Idee wurde im Jahr 1990 wieder aufgenommen, und zwar mit der Veröffentlichung eines zweiten Buchs mit Bildern des Wettbewerbs Proffesional Photographers Of America Loan Collection (Leihsammlung der professionellen Fotografen Amerikas). Über die Jahre hin wuchs die Idee von einem Buch mit einer begrenzten Anzahl von Bildern zu einer jährlichen und umfassenden Ausgabe der gesamte Leihsammlung.

1998 wurden mehrere Maßnahmen getroffen, um einen Neubeginn dieser Veröffentlichungen einzuleiten, mit Ausrichtung auf die künftigen Fortschritte der professionellen Fotografie. Die als „Leihgabe" bewerteten Bilder werden nun in einem Buch unter dem Titel PPA Loan Collection (Leihsammlung der PPA) veröffentlicht. Ein vollkommen neues Buch - PPA Showcase (PPA Schaukasten) - enthält eine Auswahl von Bildern der allgemeinen Sammlung, PPA General Collection. Beide Veröffentlichungen wurden neu designt und laufen unter neuen Namen, so daß sie visuell besser erkennbar sind und direkt mit der Identität der PPA Stroyteller (Geschichtserzähler) in Verbindung gebracht werden können.

Außerdem verstärkt PPA Showcase den pädagogischen Wert dieser Veröffentlichungen. Und, obwohl sich beide jährlichen Veröffentlichungen ergänzen, ist jedes Buch für sich alleine schon einzigartig! Die PPA Loan Collection behält ihre traditionelle Form und Größe bei, während PPA Showcase nicht nur in einem einzigartigem, neuen Format verlegt wird, sondern auch auf jeder Seite ein individuelles Bild eines Fotografen enthält.

Unsere Glückwünsche gelten nicht nur den Fotografen, deren Kreativität in diesen Veröffentlichungen präsentiert wird, sondern auch allen Fachleuten, die die Zeit und die Anstrengungen auf sich genommen haben, um am International Judging & Annual Exhibition of Professional Photography (Internationaler Wettbewerb und jährliche Ausstellung professioneller Fotografie) der PPA teilzunehmen.

Wie jeder weiß, der sich an Künstlerwettbewerben beteiligt hat, ist es nicht einfach - oder angenehm - seine Kreativität vor den Kritikern zu entblößen, aber auf lange Sicht kann das sowohl bereichernd als auch lohnend sein.

Rex Alewel, *Verleger*

脈々たる伝統の新たな幕開けにようこそ！

最初の試みとして 1978 年に *ProPhotos 1* （プロフォトズ1）が出版されて以来、PPA （プルフェッショナル・フォトグラファーズ・オブ・アメリカ）の年 1 回のコンペティションから傑出した写真を選び、永久的な印刷物の形式で発表することは、多くの写真専門家のゴールでした。1990 年、この構想は同コンペティションの写真を紹介した 2 冊目の書籍、*Professional Photographers of America Loan Collection* （プロフェッショナル・フォトグラファーズ・オブ・アメリカ・ローンコレクション）の出版により、復活しました。限られた数の写真を掲載した書籍という構想は、歳月を経て、全ローンコレクションを網羅した年 1 回の総合出版へと発展しました。

1998 年、これら出版物の新たなスタートを目指し、さらに高度なプロフェッショナルのイメージ創造に向けて焦点を再調整していき、いくつかのステップが踏まれました。「ローン」の地位が授与された写真は、現在、*PPA Loan Collection* （PPA ローンコレクション）のタイトルを付した書籍で出版されています。全く新しい第2の書籍、*PPA Showcase* （PPA ショーケース）には *PPA General Collection* （PPA ジェネラルコレクション）から選択した写真が収められています。いずれの出版物も、視覚的認識を高めて直接 *PPA Storytellers* （PPA ストーリーテラーズ）と関連付けられるよう、デザインと名称が一新されました。

PPA Showcase （PPA ショーケース）が加わったことにより、これら書籍の教育的価値が広がりました。この 2 冊の年刊書は互いに補完し合っていますが、各々がいずれもユニークな存在として独立しています。*PPA Loan Collection* （PPA ローンコレクション）は伝統的なサイズと型を保ち、一方、*PPA Showcase* （PPA ショーケース）はユニークな新形式を提供するばかりでなく、各頁に写真家 1 名の写真が掲載されています。

これら書物がその創造性を紹介している写真家各位のみならず、時間と労力を捧げ *PPA International Judging & Annual Exhibition of Professional Photography* （PPA インターナショナル・ジャッジング＆アニュアルエグジビション・オブ・プロフェッショナル・フォトグラフィー）に参加された関係者の皆様に心からお祝いの言葉をお贈りします。芸術界のコンペティションに参加した方ならご存知のように、自己の創造性を批評の下に晒すことは容易なことではありませんし、不安なことでもありますが、長期的には自己を豊かにし、恩恵をもたらすこととなるでしょう。

ありがとうございました。

Rex Alewel　（レックス・アレウェル）
出版者

為延續傳統開創了新頁而歡呼！

自從一九七八年美國專業攝影師協會首次將週年大賽的優秀作品刊印出版後，將這些傑出照片結集成書，是眾多專業攝影師追求的目標。一九九零年，輯錄參賽作品而成的第二本刊物「美國專業攝影師珍藏影集」出版，令理想再次實現。這些年來，結集成書這個構想，已從一本照片寥寥可數的小書，發展成每年出版的專業刊物—珍藏影集。

一九九八年，我們採取多項步驟，為影集創造一個新開始，重新定位把目標朝向更先進的影像表達方式。今年被選為可作珍藏的傑作，都收錄在「九八年美國專業攝影師珍藏影集」內；另外，我們選出版一本全新的「美國專業攝影師作品精選」影集，收集美國專業攝影師協會會員的其他傑出作品。兩本刊物經過重新包裝、設計和命名，是要加強視覺感觀效果，並體現美國專業攝影師以影像說故事的獨特表達方式。

「美國專業攝影師作品精選」的出現，大大加強這些刊物的教育價值。雖然這兩本攝影集互相輝映，它們各自都有其獨特之處。「九八美國專業攝影師珍藏集」仍然保留其傳統外形大小及風格，而「美國專業攝影師作品精選」不單以獨特的新形式出現，同時每頁作品更附有攝影師的照片以供參考。

我們不單衷心祝賀各位攝影師透過這些影集所表現的創意，同時也感謝所有參加者透過由美國專業攝影師協會主辦的國際專業攝影評審週年展。任何曾經參加過藝術作品比賽的人都知道，要將自己的作品顯示人前公開接受評審並不容易；但無論如何，長遠來說，多賽能增添姿彩，而我們也收獲豐碩。

出版人

艾立和

A WORD FROM THE PUBLISHER

Welcome to a new beginning of a continuing tradition!

Presenting outstanding images from PPA's annual competition in a permanent, printed format has been a goal of many photographic professionals since the very first effort—*ProPhotos 1*—was published in 1978. The idea was renewed in 1990 with the publication of a second book to feature images from this competition, *Professional Photographers Of America Loan Collection.* Over the years the idea has grown from a book with a limited number of images, to an annual comprehensive publication of the entire loan collection.

1n 1998, several steps have been taken to create a fresh start for these publications, re-focusing them toward the further advancement of professional image-making. Images awarded "loan" status are now published in a book entitled *PPA Loan Collection.* An entirely new second book—*PPA Showcase* — contains a selection of images from the PPA General Collection. Both publications have been redesigned and re-named, to strengthen their visual recognition and link them directly with the PPA *Storytellers* identity.

The addition of *PPA Showcase* expands the educational value of these publications. And, although the two annual publications compliment each other, each book now also stands alone as unique! *PPA Loan Collection* retains its traditional size and shape, while *PPA Showcase* is not only offered in a unique new format, it also features one photographer's individual image on each page of the book.

Our sincere congratulations are extended, not only to all those photographers who's creativity is featured in these publications, but to all the image makers who haven taken the time and exerted the effort to participate in PPA's *International Judging & Annual Exhibition of Professional Photography.* As anyone who has ever entered in an artistic competition knows, it is not an easy—or comfortable—task to bare one's creativity to critique; however, in the long run, it can be both enriching and rewarding.

Sincerely,

Rex Alewel

Rex Alewel, *Publisher*

Lorraine Kephart • Madisen

David Peters • Free Spirit

Patrick Abel • A Born Leader

Ian Murray • Can't Catch Me

Barry Rankin • California Dreamer

Ross Kelly • Carolina Sunrise

Hugh R. Jacob • Reflections Of Life

William Baumgartner • My Brother, My Sister, My Friend

William Baumgartner • Precious Ge

Kirk Voclain • Sister, Sister

George N. Balthazar • A Moment Of Solitude

Edwin Faller • Something Borrowed

Susan Hoermann • A Timeless Feeling

Kevin Brown • Cathedral Of Admiration

Yoshinori Hayashi • Let's Start To Bright Future

Jeffrey H. Mantler • Portal Of Love

Doug Gifford • Pyramid Of Passion

John F. Henry • Tender Moment

Michael Skerry • Blue Heaven

John Ritter • Enchanted Eveni

Peter Simmons • Timeless

Peter A. Simmons

Heidi Mauracher • Twilight Princess

Gail Nogle • Lavender Blue

Lisa Murphey • Dress Rehearsal

Audrey Wancket • Pink Latté

Linda Lapp-Murray • Welcome, Newborn

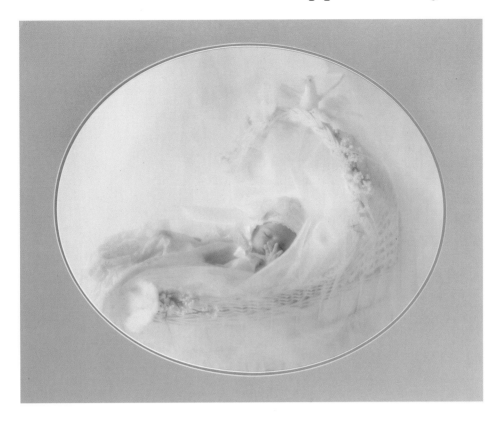

Barbara Grabill • Little One's Bath

Linda Johnson • Bookends

Joseph Campanellie • Seaside Blues

Scott Dupras • Austin's Debut

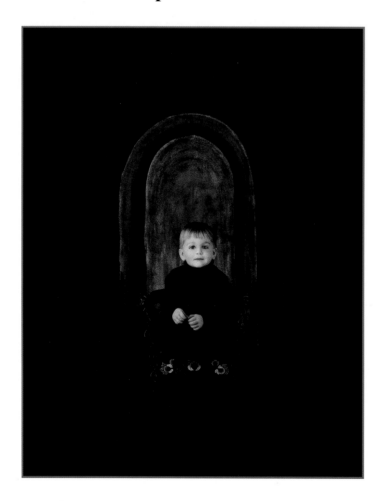

Lewis Kincheloe • Placa Rosa

Richard Newell Jr. •Alone

Gregory Daniel • Left Out

Roxanne Pearson • A Teddy Bear Affair

Richard Barnes • Dog-Gone-It

Ronald E. Jankun • Gorgeous…Simply Gorgeous

Pati Heydorn • For A Kiss

Randy Davison • Hey Mom Quick Look At Nick

Beverly Walden • Eye Of The Storm

Timothy Walden • His Father's Eyes

Michael Bell • Silent Sentry

Michael McKown • Weathering The Storm

Lynn Brown • Crystal Cathedral

Andrew Ulicki • Alpine Utopia

Roger Meritt • A Reflection At Pemaquid

Ralph O. Richter • Waimea Canyon

Stephen Palen • Autumn Morn

Robert L. Harris, Jr. • Twilight; Comet Hale-Bopp

Anthony P. Maddaloni • Thunderstorm Badlands, SD

Larry Weaver • A Time Remembered

Deborah Kreimborg • God's Pasture

Larry Scherling • The Little White Cloud

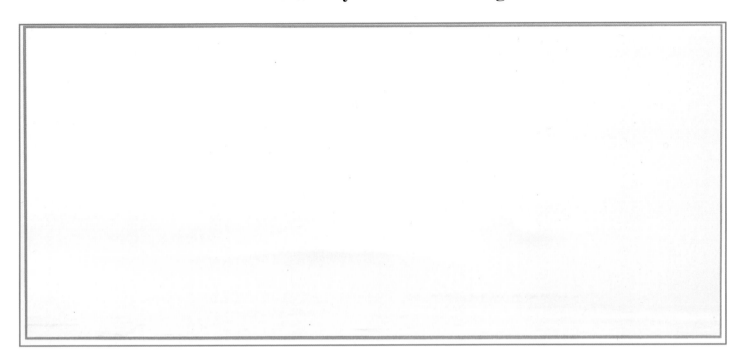

Patricia Beltrami • Winter Storm

John M. Murray • Dance In The Wind

Robert Hughes • A Reflection of Love

Robert Hughes • A Walk In The Clouds

Michael Skerry • Winter Wonderland

Dale P. Hansen • Yippi Yi Yeah

Barbara Yonts • Whispers Of Love

Jon Erickson • Beautiful Elegance

Claude J. Gagnon • Fascination

Donna Estes • Satin Roses & Silk Magnoli

John F. Richnavsky • Wedding Winds

Rick Ferro • Delicate Curves

William Duncan • Angel

Dwaine Horton • Majestic Bride

Luis Manuel Arregoitia • Over The Edge

Sally J. Perkins • Granite And Grace

Sara Frances • Age Of Elegance

Tony Estevez • Princesa Bella

Jesus A. Cabrera • Someday

Tony Limeres • From Past To Future

Butch Stark • Prelude To The Moment

Dori Arnold • Pretty In Pink

Audrey Wancket • Any Moment

Barbara White • Pretty Miss

Randy G. Fraley • Alone And Forgotten

Beverly Walden • Captured Innocence

Timothy Walden • Age Of Innocence

John Bergman • Party Girls

Lisa Murphey

Midnight Rodeo

Tiger Lily

Sirene

Scott Dupras • Spell Bound

Carrie Evenson • The Look Of Love

Steve Lopushinsky • Someone's Watching Over Me

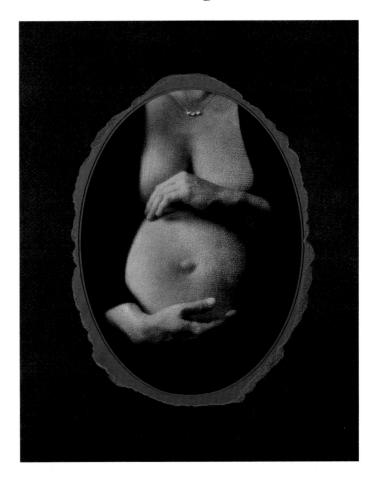

Louise Simone • Metamorphosis

Joyce Wilson • La Femme

James Frederick • Hidden

James Wyant • The Mirror In Grandma's Attic

James Frederick • Hidden

Keith Sturch • In The House Where No One Laughs

Steve Kozak • Simple Pleasures

Rich Voorhees • Striking

James Stevens • Veiled Tragedy

Jon Johnson • The First Snow

IB Larsen • Scandinavian Winter

S u z a n n e   C .   F i s c h e r • Scouting The Way

S u s i e   F l e m m i n g • Life's Simple Pleasures

F u z z y   D u e n k e l • Haunted

Ferdinand Neubauer • Beginning A Fairy Tale

City Hideaway

Corlin Quick • Our Castle

Paul Tsang • The Wave Of Love

Lisa Lamping • Sands Of Time

Donald Cianci • Together We... Can

Theodore A. Wagner • Sailing Home

Robert L. Stewart • Snake River Overlook

Brian Baer • The Sky Is Not The Limit

Kenny Simmons • The Great Smoky Mountains

Steven T. Emmerich • Winter's Wrath

Charlie Rees • Evening Sail

Garrett Nose • Mirage

Karen Bates • How Sweet It Is

Neal H. Clipper • Two Hot Dogs, Hold The Mustard

Nizam Mohamed • Love Makes The World Go Round

David Tompkins • Romance In Saint Patrick's Cathedral

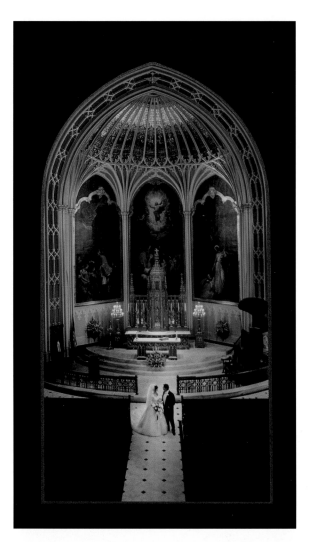

Donna Abshire • Timeless Elegance

James Travers • End Of A Perfect Day

Ron Carroll • Elegant Romance

Sae Lee • Eternal River

Michael Fant • Avocet Elegance

Colorful Getaway

James R. Stagner • Serenity

Jim LaSala • Birth Of A Flower

Augusts Upitis • Morning Pearls

Bogdan J. Fundalinski • The Awakening Of Spring

Susan Kopecky • Primary Presentation

Lynne Damianos • Sunflower Sunset

Harry W. Carter • Eccentric Kaleidoscope

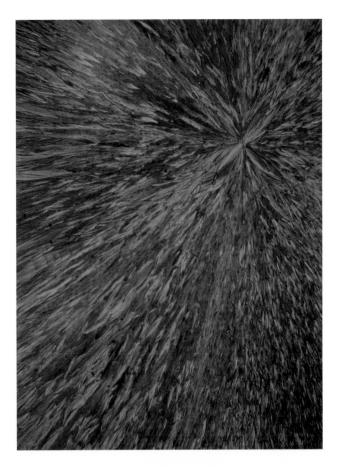

Helen Yancy • Vortex Of Silence

Harry W. Carter • Cascading Crystals

Brian Baer • Arms Of Aspiration

Dwight Okumoto • Family Ties

Dave Swoboda • Dimensions

Mindy Hesslink • Hurry Home

Richard Cunningham • Hoop Dreams

Tjhang Piauw Tjong • Sensuality

Jemmy Iskandar • Victorian Brid

Tjhang Piauw Tjong • Sleeping Beauty

Djoni Paulus • Always Close To You

Kitty Reedorf • For Better Or Worse

Deborah Brackmann • I Got You Babe

Bernardo Restrepo • Hey Guys Play A Song For Us

Jeffrey Rose • Glenn Sullivan

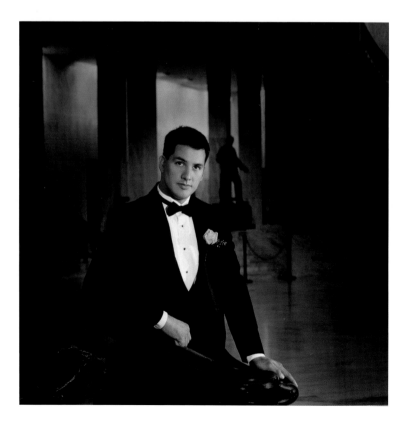

Ken Taylor • Solitary Moment

F r a n k   S a l a s • A Feeling Of Beauty

Jerry Small • A Kiss Before The Storm

Frank Cricchio • You and Me Against The World

John Kornachuk • Touched By An Angel

Larry Capdeville • Enchanted

Steven Bergano • Enchanted Moment

David Derex • The Producer David Brown

B.C. Baggett • Eye On The Future

Oscar Lozoya • Vidra

Marilyn Purvis • Sweet Dreams

Larry Scherling • A Penny For Your Thoughts

David Dern • Windows To The Soul

Sandy Fraley • Cherish The Child

Barbara Yonts • Come Play With Me

Chris Carlson • Innocence

Ron Richards • I Believe I Can Fly

Polly Crumley • Curiosity

Lee Larsen • Oh My!

Maria Martins • My Bear

74   PPA LOAN COLLECTION

Tom McDonald • Lost In A Dream

James Reese • Gam Paw's Girl

Mary T. Tracy • Dough Baby

Rick Donhauser • Book Sales

John Teague • Croissant Chaos

James T. Wentink Jr. • Eye See You

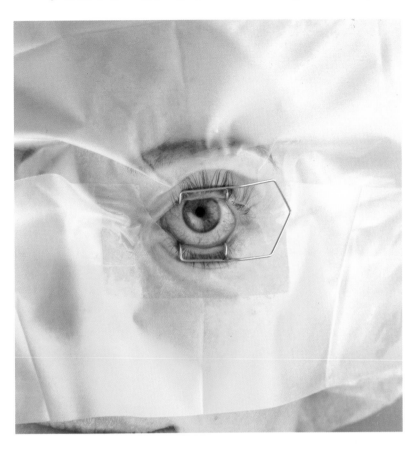

Till Hezel • Stir Fry

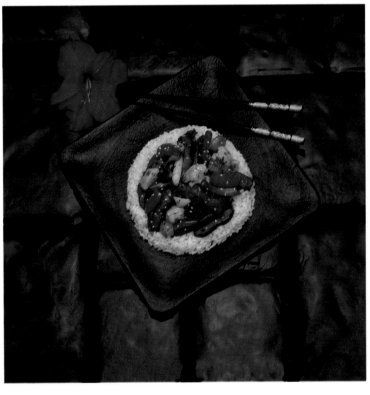

Mark Allen Wright • Technical Merit

Dennis Harding • Going Home

Richard Carpenter • An October Moment

Cindy Kassab • Sunflowers Everywhere

Jacqueline Baldini • Misty Rose

Juan Aragon • Unseen Blossom

Shirley E. Green • Grandma's Favorites

Linda Huddle Martin • The Long Way Home

Rachael Weekley • Innocence

Ken Whitmire • Down Home

Martin Miller • Little Wonders

Mark Spencer • Wonderland

Richard A. Bass • Hay Seed

Dustine Wallace • Diddy-up Towboy

Lisa Luedtke • Freedom

Paul Nysetvold • Watchful Eye

Mark Haskell • Hey What's He Looking At

Gary Weitzeil • Midnight Sun

Tim Mathiesen • City Of Angels

Gary Thibeault • Grand Pequot Tower Lobby

Jeffrey Jacobs • St. Mary's Auditorium

Neil Bolton • Interior #1

Jeffrey Jacobs • Promus-Call Center

Seraphina Landgrebe • Watchers Of The Wood

Arvind Vallabh • Dancing In Heaven

Glenn F. Hohnstreiter • Moment Of Glory

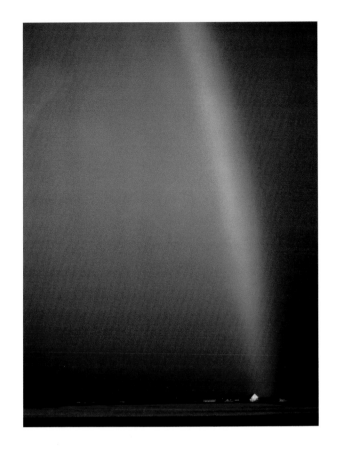

Dwight Smith • Fire In The Sky

ames Carney • Tears Of A Mountain

John D. Wacker • Good To The Last Drop

John F. Henry • Surf's Up

David Bayles • Koi Fish

Gerald Harvey • Five Of A Kind

Chris Beltrami • Playing Hooky

Janet Bonsall • Follow Through

Kiyomi Hayashi • Bright Autumn All Weather

Duane Sauro • A Stroll In Time

Fuzzy Duenkel • Guenevere

Mark Spencer • Roots

Susan Torregrosa • I Will Be Waiting For Thee

Gayle Tewksbury Tiller • Wave Dancer

Tina Marie Vance • Childhood Treasures

Steven Ahrens • Emily

Carla Nelms • Heirloom Innocence

Donald Butler Jr. • Snow White

Allen Austin • 97 Bride

Laurence Seidman • Jackie

Rick Staudt • Maybe Daddy Was Right

Emily Blom Carroll • Wistfully Waiting

Peter Dyer • Long Wait Over

Kelly Blosser • Balance And Grace

James H. Hayes III • Graced In Tradition

Robert Lino • Spiral To Happiness

Josephine Schoepfer • Timeless Beauty

Kem McDaniels • Yesterday's Bride

Robert Ruymen • Your Day Will Come

Peggy Sue Seehafer • They Call Him Tornado

Don Busath • Wagon Train

Genaro Castelan • The Plough Man

Douglas J. Wright • Evening Crossing

John Bergman • Rooms With A View

Joan E. Stewart • Sea Urchins

Russ Hanson • The Grain Grows On

Susan Michal • Montana Mist

Jake Fish • The Hour Of The Wolf

Darlyn Davison • Awesome Eyes

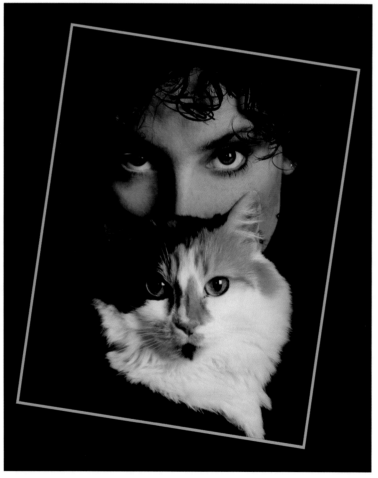

Paul Tsang • A Glance Of The Eye

John Perryman • Altamaha Swamp

Steven T. Emmerich • Emerald Pool

Susan Michal • The Hills Are Alive

Art Cashmere • Up In Arms

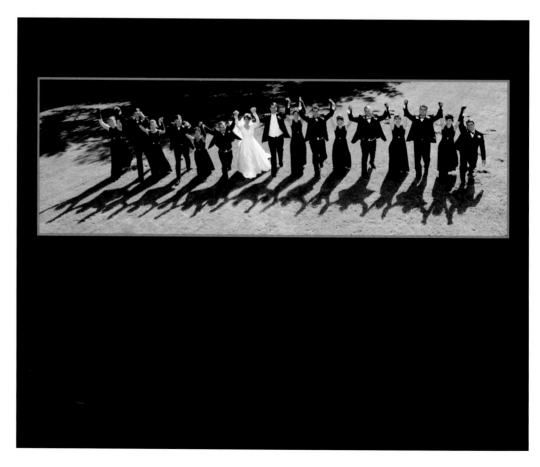

Robert Kunesh • Genesis

Paul Tsang • Fall In Love

Robert Lino • The Proposal

JoLene Hum • Attitudes

Gordon Underwood • Autumn Heritage

David G. Wacker • The Golden Years

Kevin Barry • Follow Me

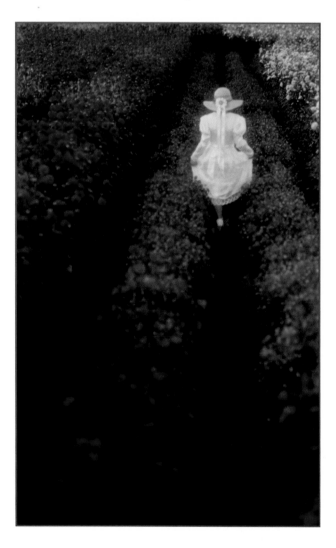

Yuki Hayashi • Look For The Autum

Linda Davies • Weathered By Time

Patricia Beltrami • The Final Turn Towards Home

Michael Galetto • A Silent Cry

Kathryn Sommers • Mad About Yo

Andrew Ulicki • Rainy Day Blues

Paula Hawkins • Myself In The Mirror

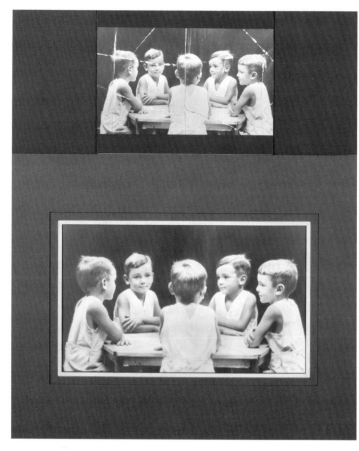

Angela Meulemans • My Three Little Angels

Marlene Loria • For The Cover

Linda Weaver • Jacob

Jo Burkhardt • Laddie

Linda Weaver • Hannah

Maria Martins • Wind Beneath My Wings

Steve Mackley • And She Wept

Robert Jenks • Sightless Motion

Brian Schmitt • The Calm Before The Storm

Jim Binegar Jr. • Summer Splendor

Marie M. Curtis • Birch Bark Tattoos

Alan Spitznagle • Faded Dreams

Mel Martin • On The Move

Charles A. Parker • Spring Ice

Lou Mudd • Desert Rose

Jane Walsh • Pause On A Misty Morning

Kathy J. Wierda • Montana Gold

Beverly Toves • Repose

Carrie Evenson • Sheer Beauty

Carrie Evenson • Beautiful Dreamer

J e f f   L o c k l e a r • Companionship

R i c h a r d   B e i t z e l • And Then We Went Home

Mary Anne Ricks • True To His Nature

Janice Johnson • Rapid Action

Russell L. Hansen • The Game Of Life Don't Play It Alone

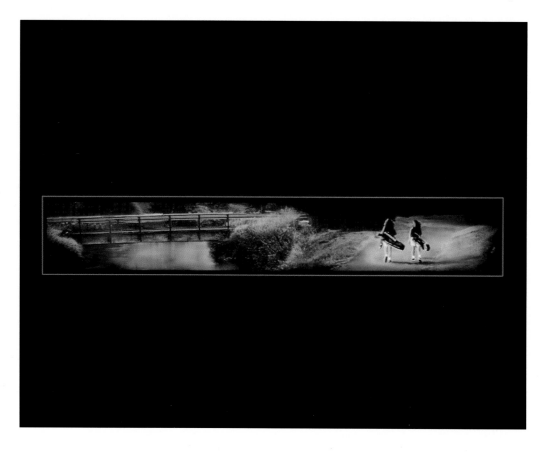

Christopher Kimble • Sharing A Moment

Loy A. Payne • The Golf Lesson

Dwight Smith • Sonoran Morning

Robert Hughes • Three Brothers

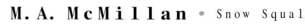

M.A. McMillan • Snow Squal

Jack Foley • Dog Day Afternoon

Sharon Baker • Lucifer's Lure

Daniel Thornton • Impressions

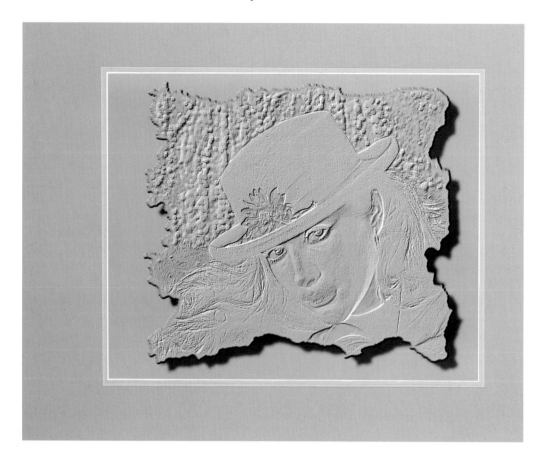

Robert Hughes • The Loss

Tim Mathiesen • High, Wide, Spectacular

Kelly Scheimberg • Planetscape

Mark K. Kunstman • Safeway Up And Around

Cathy Sherman • That's Life

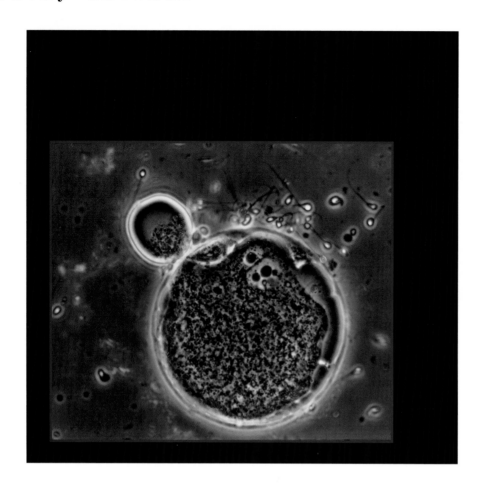

Charles A. Parker • Midnight Blue

Richard Martin • Cyber Madness

Gary McMullen • State-Of-The-Art

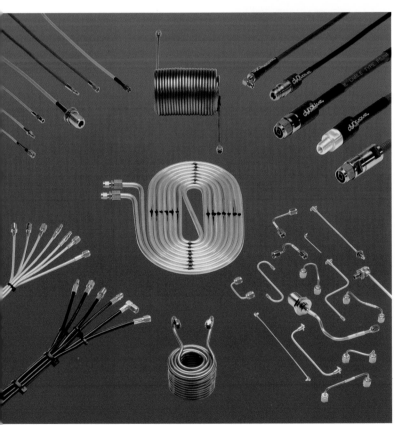

Lynne Damianos • Dynawave Connectors

Light Fantasies

Bob Kahn • Style And Grace

Indra Leonardi • Melody Of Love

Indra Leonardi • Shanghai Bride

Indra Leonardi • Classique Beauty

Kitty Reedorf • The Color Of Love

John Molnar • My Daddy

Betty Huth • The Circle Of Love

Edward Booth • Stairway To A New Beginning

Mary Beavers • Christy And Shawn

James Schmelzer • The Main Event

Dennis Mock • Carol And Michael November 23, 1997

Buddy M. Stewart • One Floor From Heaven

Jeffrey Rose • Love Leads The Way

Bernardo Restrepo • Our Love Lights The House Of God

Ronald Kotar • The Grandeur Of Love

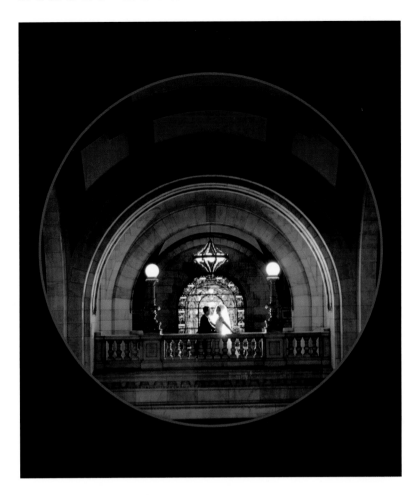

Patrick Rice • Swept Away

Ladd Scavnicky • Gothic Passion

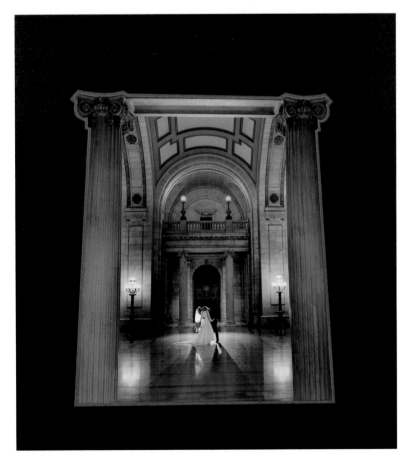

Sandy Sahagian • Where Land Meets The Sky

Alexandra Schaefer Hees • Natural Phenomenon

Peter Paul Rubens • Ebb Tide

Pamela Anne Dyer • Reflective Sunrise

Anthony P. Maddaloni • Golden Orifice

Dennis Martin • Garden Of The Gods

Brian Schmitt • Hardworking Harvest

Daniel Stoller • Dad's Evening Excursion

Genaro Castelan • Violent Eruptions

Kelly Richards • Monolith

Edgar W. Matuska • I Am The Artistic Director

Jose Alvarez • Ramon

Hud Andrews • Graphic Designer

Fredrick Ramseyer • Honest Day's Work

Karin B. Fetzner • Story Teller

Cherilyn Nocera • The Next Picasso

John F. Richnavsky • Ebony And Ivory

Jerry Huffman • The Guitar Player

Timothy Walden • Fender Bender

Jose Alvarez • Daniel

Scott Nozawa • Music Is My Life

James Kim Han • A Dream Of Love

Colleen Drew • A Moment of Solitude

William O'Halloran • A Kiss To Build A Dream On

Gary Fagan • Everything's Okay

Steven Henriques • Wrapped Up In Your Love

Irvin Yamada • Ocean Mist Of Love

Julie Robillard • Immortality

Garrett Nose • Ebb Tide

Bruce Hudson • Are You Sure You Saw (A) Whale?

4/11/99/

Jerry W. Venz • The Hurley Family

Oscar Lozoya • Jugando Con La Muerte (Playing With Death)

Barry Hayes • The Contenders

Linda Weaver • Profile Of Poverty

Oscar Lozoya • Eyes Of Winter

Sally Merritt Swart • A Mile In My Shoes

Jim Robideau • Window To The Past

Edgar Lobit Jr. • Dusty Serengetti Trails

Larry Weaver • Peace In The Valley

Lynn A. Damon • The Grand Canal

Stephen E. Klemm • 42 Coupe

Richard Bell • BSA-3

Richard Bell • Monetti Pens

Curt Ullery • Pen And Pencil

arry Finlay • Whirlpool Sculpture

William Piacesi • Comfort

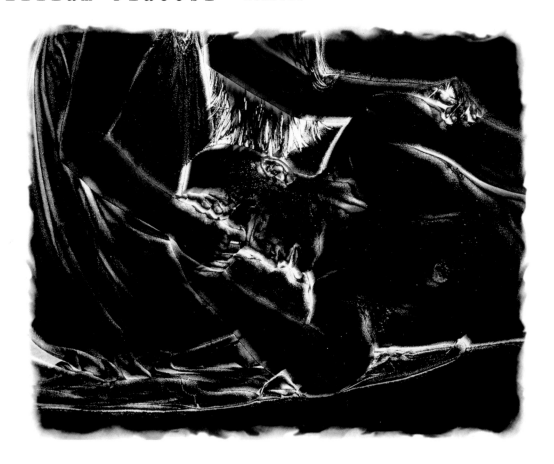

John Nelson • In Her Wildest Dreams

Richard Rader • Passage Through O'Hare

Daniel Stoller • Thee Gathering Place

Timothy Walden • The Aristo-Crab

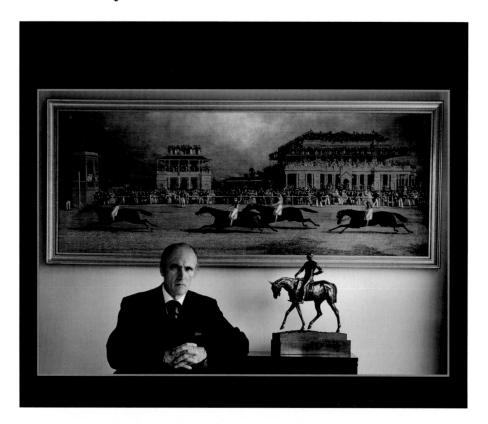

Joe Derocher • Solitude

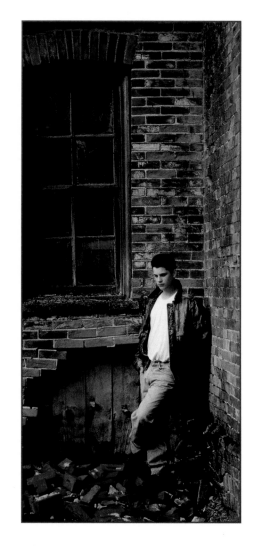

Ron Stewart • Kurt – Wedding Day Portrait

Richard May • Imitation Of Solitude

Mille Totushek • A Man Of Few Words

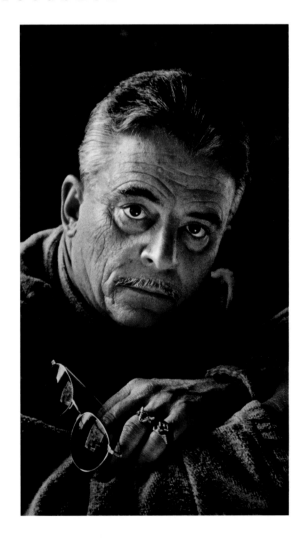

Marvin Asher • Runaway

Sandy Fraley • The Lookout

Linda Motzko • Enchanted Passage

Peter Ellis • The Love I Lost

Angelica Conley • Solace At Sunset

Genaro Castelan • The Survivor

Susan H. Johnson • Sun Catchers

David H. Davis • Standing With The Wind

Robert Mock • Floating Fantasy

Michael LaCour • Crimson Sunset

Thom Rouse • Paper Shuffle

Bill Smith • Furnace Fire Works

Bob Cleere • The Mask

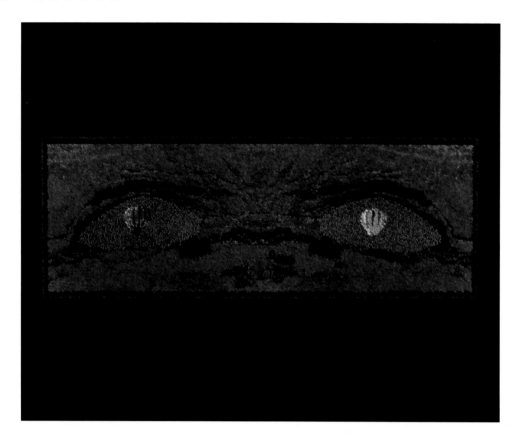

Michael Sohns • Appointment With Destiny

Dale P. Hansen • Lost In Time

Dominic Iodice • Introducing LXY and LXZ

Dcalictric

LXV PR#3

Mark Allen Wright • Yellow Roadster

Matthew Owen • From Fantasy To Reality

John Currens • Blue Thunde

Gene Gabelli • Manhattan Bridge

Carl Lindbloom • Passage To A Dream

Trudy Lom-Ourada • The Deep Blue

Jeanine Cragin • Look What The Stones Washe

Lindsey Nichols • All Creatures Great & Small

Michael Ayers

Kent Miller • Moody Blue

William Stevenson • The Choir Master

Dave Newman • Wisdom

Roger Tamm • The Lord Is My Ligh

Randy McNeilly • Head Of The Class

Scott Smith • The Mentalist

Dave Montizambert • Lord Of The Violin

Douglas J. Wright • Wood Sculptor

James Frieze • Attitude

Lisa Lamping • Come And Get Me

Rick Avalos • Saturday Morning Routine

Carl Caylor • Intense Perspective

Charles Green • Kingsley's List

David Pixley • Loves Embrace

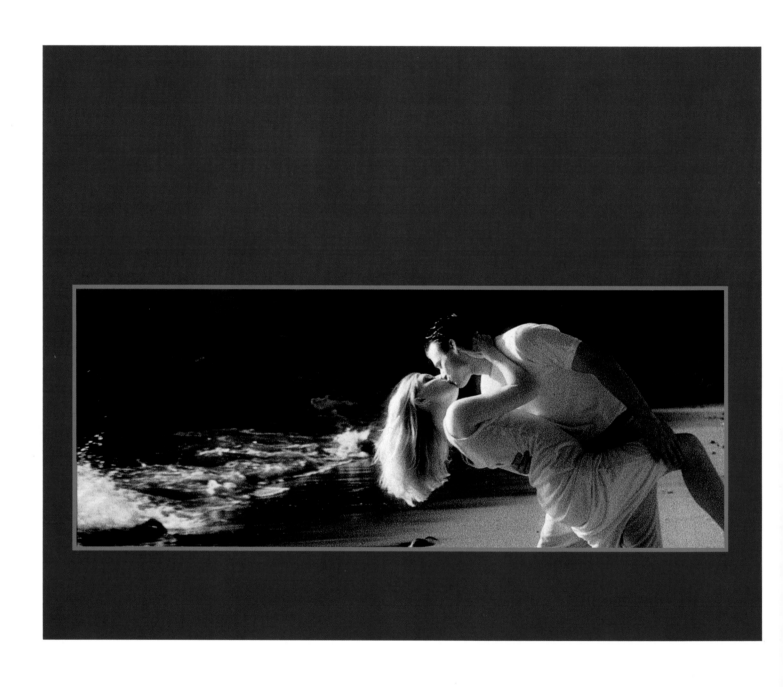

Kay Eskridge • Portrait Of A Children's Photographer

Jon Johnson • Out Of The Blue

Jon Johnson • Hi Tech In Blue

Kay   Saladin • Jacob – Red Striped Shirt

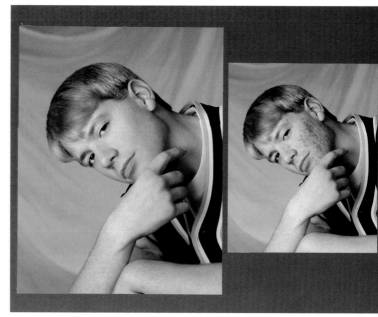

Scott   Stegman • Gets The Red Out

Cheryl   Hibbard • Joseph

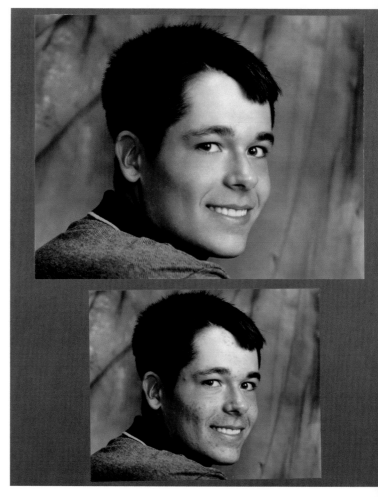

Nema Velia • Mac

Cheryl Hibbard • Joel

Marlene Loria • Isabella

Cindy Tiefenbrunn • Dave

George Smith • The Estate Sisters

Vaughn Hendrie • A Day With Great Grandpa

Ronald Nichols • Enough To Share

David G. Wacker • Good Morning My Love

John Perryman • Autumn Splendor

Beverly Ann Jenkins • Misty Morning Mansion

Bill Dasher • Hula Bowl Half Time

Marcia Wright Tomchay • Bad Habits

Sam, keep the fire burning!   Greg McCanless

Greg McCanless • Treasured Moments

Ian Murray • Dance Class

Steven Winslow • Extended Elegance

Felice Boucher • Adam & Eve

Jeffery DeLaney • And They Prayed…

William Lind • All Together Again

John Riddell • He's Mine All Mine

M.A. McMillan • Drummer

Gordon Underwood • Etched

John L. Shipman • The Magic Is In The Hands

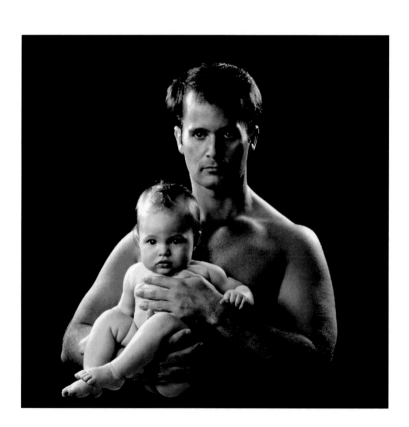

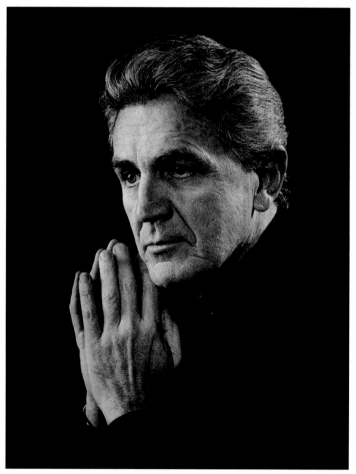

Mary McNeilly • Embrace

Victoria Austin Powell • Toot, Toot, Toot

Nancy Wood • 1, 2, 3, Out

Helen Murin • I Still Love You Grandma

Lee Larsen • Carrie

Marie Quick • Little Mona Lisa

Ken Lunderby • Second Hand Rose

Anna Marie Kane • Italian Wedding

John Solano • Renee And Pau

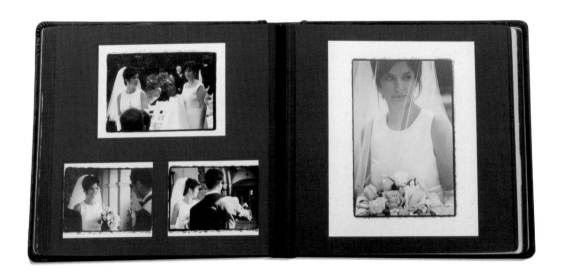

Terry L. Walburg • A Tale Of Two Hearts

Kristine Salmore • Reflections On Motherhood

Yasutaka Kajiyama • Quiet

Masayuki Hasegawa • My Memorial Day

Mike Scott • Profile Of Love

Norihisa Koshino • White Wedding Cup

Norihisa Koshino • Water Fall With A Brid

Chris Beltrami • A July 4th Wedding

Ralph Melvin • When Two Become One

Stanley Rhoden • Angela And Rich

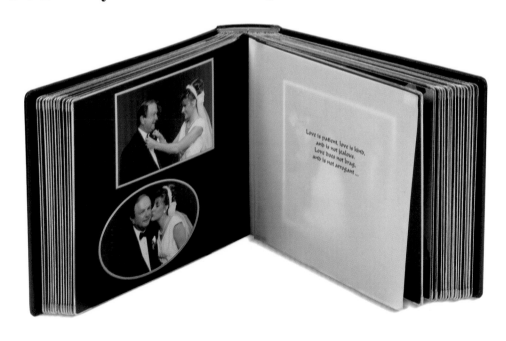

Steve Roundy • Sundown Stop-Off

Ken Whitmire • My Golden Hour

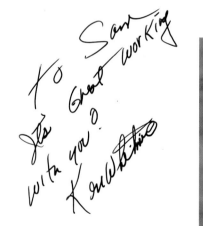

Michael Timmons • Misty Morning Interlude

Paul Prince • Child's Play

Bill Dasher • The Long Walk Home

Su Kaye • Flight Path

John Graupmann • Old World Charm

Daniel Thornton • A Test Of Time

Jim Chamberlain • Monet's Garden

Larry Dean • Out Of Time

PERIKA'S
STUFF

TRANSFORMS WICKER INTO A PIECE OF ART

Monica Farah
Perika's Stuff Transforms Wicker
Into A Piece Of Art

Lu Yu • Our Life

Angela Meulemans • Dressed For The Holidays

Lisa Luedtke • The Beauty Beyond

Duane Sauro • Statuesque

David M. Deutsch • A Moment Of Solitude

David M. Deutsch • The Arrogance Of Youth

John F. Souza • Steppin Out

Steven Ahrens • Sisters

Stephen Rudd • Vertical Elegance

Armando Rojas • Communion

Scott Dupras • Diamond In The Rough

Norman L. Rehme • Vintage Velvet

Deborah Hoff • Tri Power

B. C. Baggett • Global Service

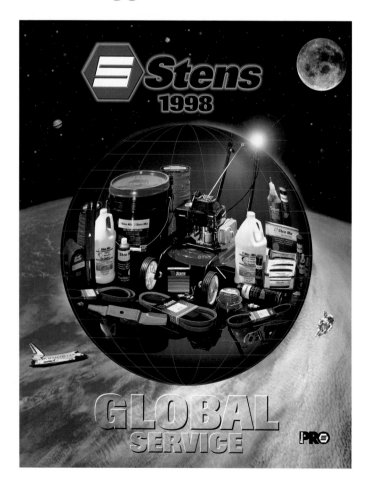

Matthew Owen • Elegant Irons

Steven T. Emmerich • Modified Designs

Tom Collins • The Invaders

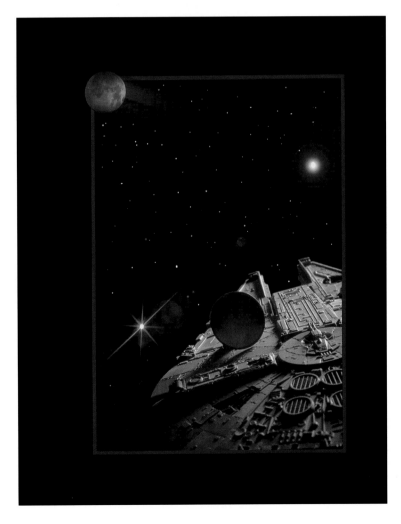

Doran Wilson • Stamping Die

Don Romero • Cool Blue

Don Romero • Mucho Caliente

Max Toro • My Favorite Spot

Till Hezel • Welcome To The Bates' Motel

Gary Thibeault • Foxwoods Resort Casino

Jeffrey Jacobs • Courtyard At Dawn

T. Paul Miller • Sunset Over Cinci

Robin Ewing • Jack And The Box

Robin Ewing • Evening With White Zinfandel

Thom Rouse • Secret Of The Pharaohs

216 PPA LOAN COLLECTION

David Ratcliff • Wild Onions

John Currens • XRay Shoe

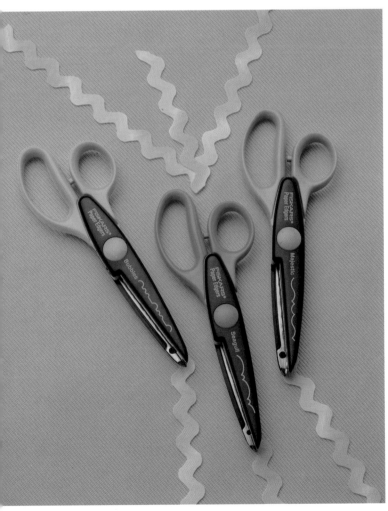

Stephanie Broome • Designer Edges

Su Kaye • Step Out Of The Window

Basilio Perez Perez • La Historia Del Uino

Dennis Fraise • Vintage Collector

Kathi Rapini • Red Moons Rising

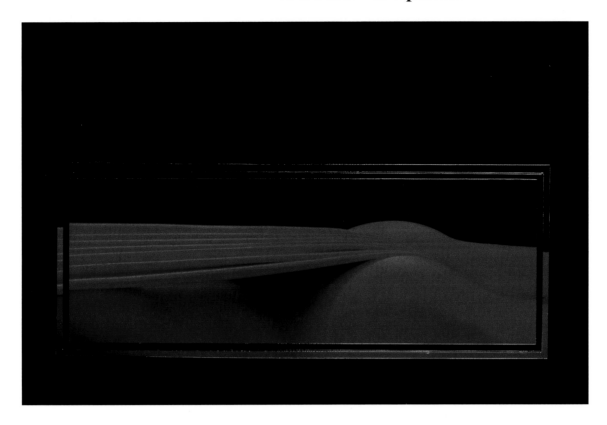

Robert E. Handley • Eastern Mystique

Darton Drake • Show Girl

Sandra Carney • Consoling

Randy Houdashelt • Wrapped In Her Thoughts

Kenneth Long • Shades Of Passion

Gene Lista • Scarecrow

Susan Weyenberg • Sidewalk Soloist

Jo Burkhardt • Eternal Spring

Robert Faust • Great Great Grandparents

Dot Brogan-Bowen
Grandmother's Twins

Susan Martin-Lemmen
Victorian Charm

Beth Tobias • Sugar Everything Nice

Valerie Markle • Sitting Pretty

Audrey Wancket • Dog Gone Harvest

Kent Krueger • Eyes Of Sadness

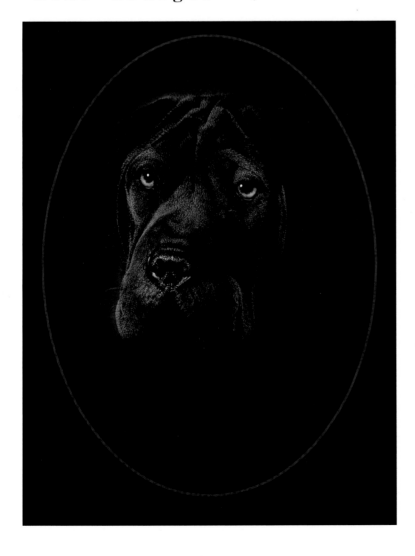

Joan E. Stewart • Spike

Jacquelyn Lloyd • Opposites Attract

Kelly Scheimberg • Fishing Fleet

Anthony P. Maddaloni • Morning Light North Rim

Dennis Kirkpatrick • Tranquility

Robert Dantoni • Irish Country Road

Deborah Billingsley • Quiet Reflection

Mary Anne Ricks • Serenity

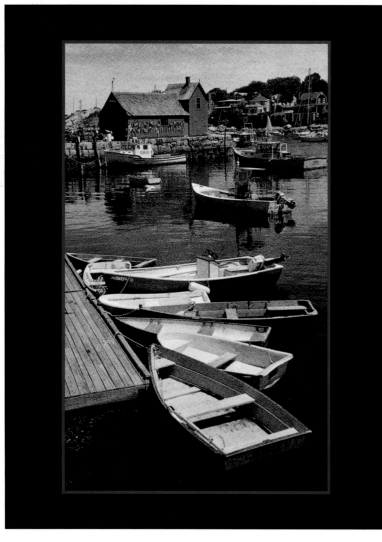

James T. Lawson • Boats At Motif #1

Mollie Isaacs • Silent Swimmer

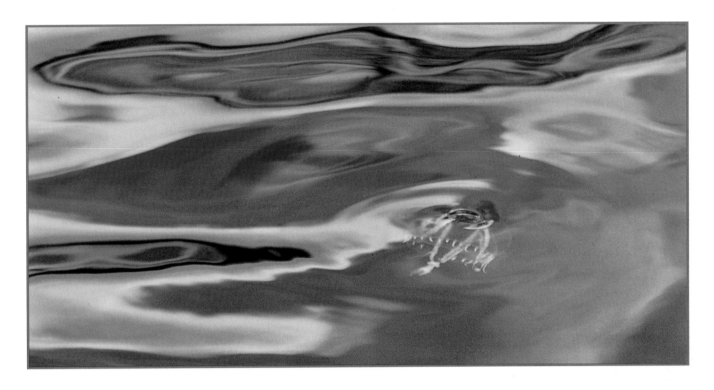

Bob Cleere • Cool Mountain Stream

Jean A. Wacker • Makes You Sneeze

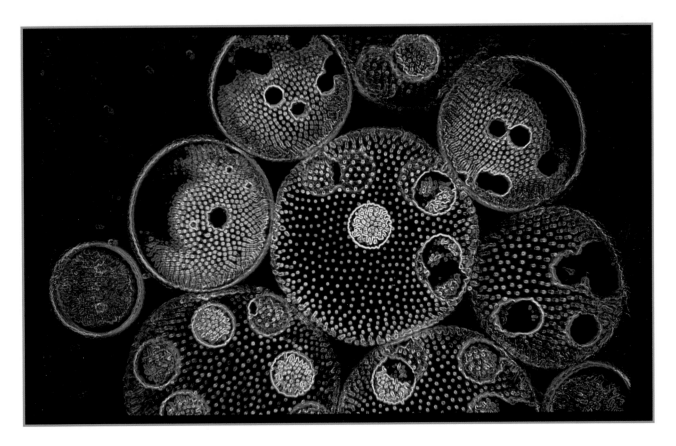

Ken Meade • Primary Crystal

Dwight Smith • Primary Composition

Fredrick Ramseyer • Crystal Moment

Denny Rice • True Blue

Brad McMullin • Elegance

T. Paul Miller • Liquid Steel

Alan Weinerman • Endless Threads

Steven Ing Ming Sioe • Crystal Ball Chain

Robin Ewing • Persistence Of Light

Evening Of Romance

Tom Collins • Kiss The Sky

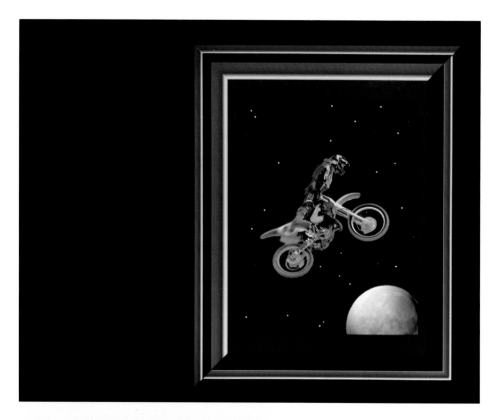

Russell L. Hansen • Womanscycle

Sandy Sahagian • Journey's End

Jake Fish • A Pledge Of Allegiance

Abel Castelan • Tears Of Life

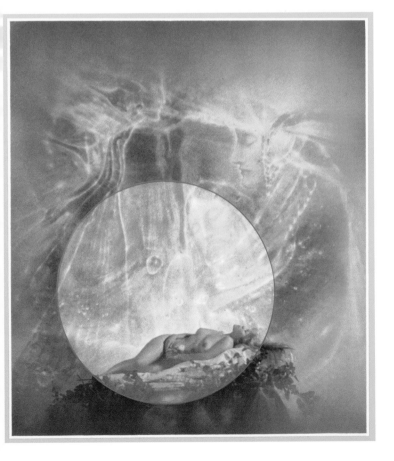

Jim Fender • Died For Our Sins

Charles A. Parker • Seeds Of Opportunity

Jim Fender • Personal Vortex

David Moss • Showoff

Dennis G. Schwartz • Dairy-Aire

Walter Klages • Warm Memories

John Lui • The Love Between Two Generations

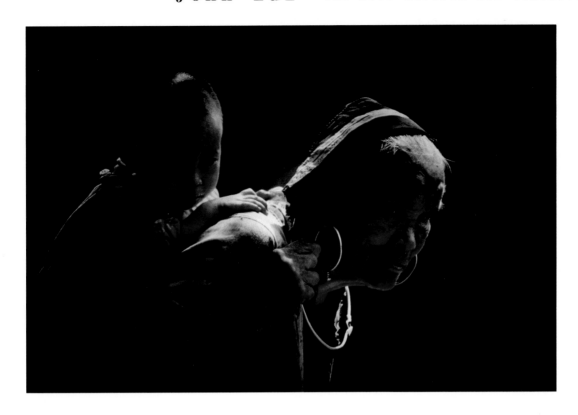

David Dern • All Dressed Up – No Place To Go

Ed Lausch • Stitch Of Time

B u d d y   M.   S t e w a r t • Rapunzel

C h e r i l y n   N o c e r a • Generation X

T o m   M o n a h a n • Touch Of Country

D o u g l a s   W o l f e • Fallen Angel

Hope Scarff • The Phantom Artist

L C Moore • Angles And Curves

Barry Rankin • William's Way

Scott Dupras • Amanda

Elizabeth Cruger • Balance

Tom Collins • Ballet

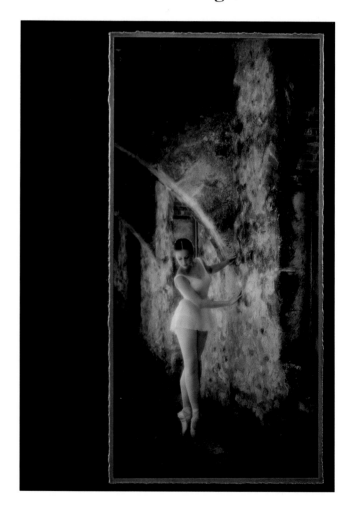

244 PPA LOAN COLLECTION

Duane Sauro • Flowers In The Attic

Fuzzy Duenkel • Back Porch Blues

William Piacesi • When Darkness Comes

Jesus A. Cabrera • Summer Love

Dennis Wells • Radiant Day

Hun Kim • An Aroma Of Roses

Michael Ayers • All I Ask Of You

John Michael Hannan Jr. • Julianna And Jared's Love Story

Paul Bernstein • Brian's Bar Mitzvah

Eric Wittmayer • Amy And Bruce October 12, 1997

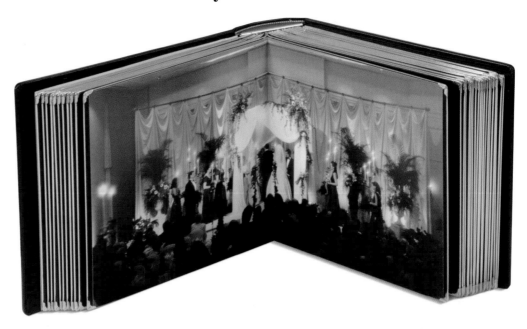

James H. Hayes III • Leslie And Steve

Philip D. Brent • Our Love Story

T. Paul Miller • West Minster

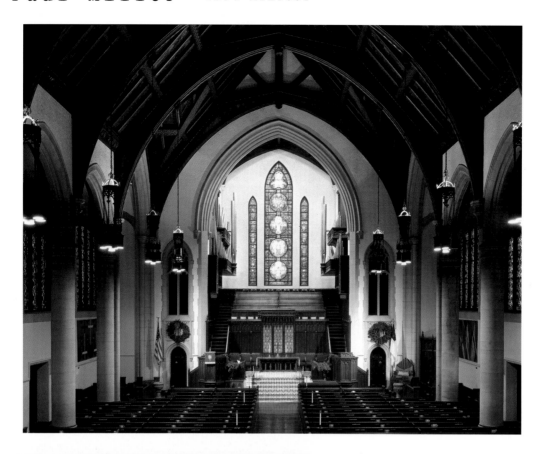

Ed Tilley • Kegg Pipe Organ Builder

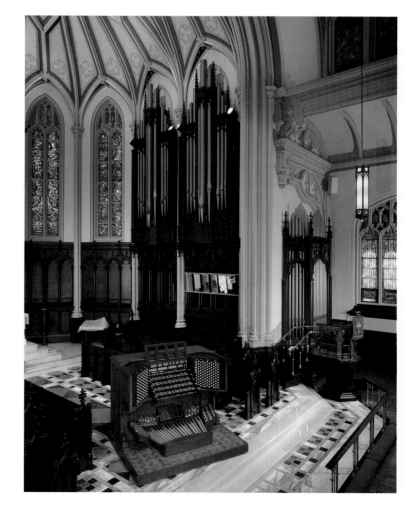

Don Romero • Gotham City

Michael Good • Cittá Di Amoré

Cindy Kassab • Sleepy Harbor

Mark A. Bohland • Fleeting Mist

Don Emmerich • Water Colors

Juan Aragon • Yellowish

Ruth Wittmayer • Blue Velvet

Debrah Muska • A Breed Apart

Debrah Muska • Mo & Flo

Pamela Setchell • Gentle Champions

Sandra Pfohl • Older Than I Wanna Be

Kay Saladin • Scar Face

Lu Yu • Nice Day

Karen Wares • Only View Available

Jurgen Lorenzen • Study In Bronze And Glass

Robert Ruymen • Sun Of God

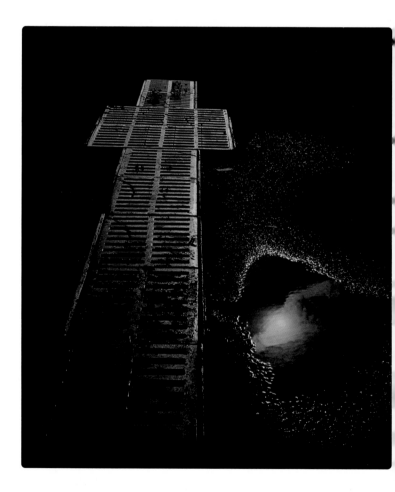

James H. Hayes III • The Bottom Line

Matthew Weston • Little Dripper

Roger Daines • Got Light

Joe McNemar • The Red Piece

Renate Pfleiderer • Nouvelle Cuisine

Richard Marchisotto • Spicy Sauce

Richard Marchisotto • Grandma's Pie

Shawn Friesner • Hot Pink Packard

Chris John Rockafellow • Mr. Hyde Lurking In The Darkness

Duane Sauro • Boss Bikes And Barmaids

Alan Weinerman • Mustang Heaven

B.C. Baggett • Dream Machines

Doug Boylan • Shaped By Nature

Jon Allyn • Composed

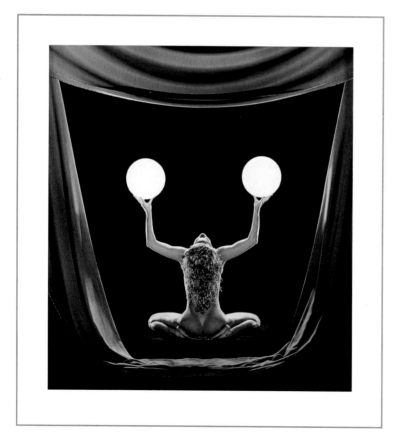

Oscar Lozoya • Mask

Robert F. Zemba • Don't Let Go

Jack Foley • The Watergirl

Denise Smith • Wash-A-Bye-Baby

Michael Ayers • Columbus Nightfall

Martha "Marty" Weinerman • New York, New York

John Marion • Dream Quenchers

Lee Skrobot • Endangered Beauty

Dirk Brouwer, Jr. • Sittin' Pretty

Ewing, Robin	Evening With White Zinfandel	C	216
Ewing, Robin	Jack And The Box	C	216
Ewing, Robin	Persistence Of Light	I	234
Hibbard, Cheryl	Joel	NEG	185
Hibbard, Cheryl	Joseph	NEG	184
Markle, Valerie	Sitting Pretty	P	224
Simmons, Kenny	The Great Smoky Mountains	I	52
Vickery, Sharon	Evening Of Romance	C	235
Vickery, Sharon	The Power Of Samsara	C	235
Wittmayer, Eric	Amy And Bruce October 12, 1997	A	249
Wittmayer, Ruth	Blue Velvet	I	253

HAWAII

Dasher, Bill	Hula Bowl Half Time	I	188
Dasher, Bill	The Long Walk Home	I	202
Henry, John F.	Surf's Up	I	92
Henry, John F.	Tender Moment	W	15
Kim Han, James	A Dream Of Love	P	152
Nose, Garrett	Ebb Tide	P	154
Nose, Garrett	Mirage	W	54
Okumoto, Dwight	Family Ties	D/RE	62
Smith, George	The Estate Sisters	P	186
Yamada, Irvin	Ocean Mist Of Love	P	154

ILLINOIS

Asher, Marvin	Runaway	I	165
Butler Jr., Donald	Snow White	W	100
Faller, Edwin	Something Borrowed	W	13
Fender, Jim	Died For Our Sins	I	237
Fender, Jim	Personal Vortex	I	238
Handley, Robert E.	Eastern Mystique	I	219
Iodice, Dominic	Dcalictric	C	173
Iodice, Dominic	Introducing LXY and LXZ	C	173
Iodice, Dominic	LXV PR#3	C	173
Jankun, Ronald E.	Gorgeous… Simply Gorgeous	P	23
Jenkins, Beverly Ann	Misty Morning Mansion	I	187
Kane, Anna Marie	Italian Wedding	A	196
Klemm, Stephen E.	42 Coupe	C	160
Meade, Ken	Primary Crystal	I	232
Nichols, Lindsey	All Creatures Great & Small	I	176
Nozawa, Scott	Music Is My Life	P	151
Purvis, Marilyn	Sweet Dreams	P	72
Rodgers, Karen	The Gift	P	43
Rouse, Thom	Secret Of The Pharaohs	C	217
Rouse, Thom	Paper Shuffle	C	171
Seehafer, Peggy Sue	They Call Him Tornado	I	104
Stewart, Ron	Kurt — Wedding Day Portrait	W	164
Taylor, David	I've Got A Secret	P	24
Thornton, Daniel	A Test Of Time	I	203
Thornton, Daniel	Impressions	D/P	132
Tracy, Mary T.	Dough Baby	P	75
Underwood, Gordon	Autumn Heritage	P	113
Underwood, Gordon	Etched	I	193
Wancket, Audrey	Any Moment	P	38
Wancket, Audrey	Dog Gone Harvest	P	225
Wancket, Audrey	Pink Latté	P	18

INDIANA

Baggett, B.C.	Dream Machines	D/P	261
Baggett, B.C.	Eye On The Future	D/P	70
Baggett, B.C.	Global Service	D/T	210
Cassidy, Steve	Famous Makers Bath	C	212
Conley, Angelica	Solace At Sunset	I	168
Hum, Jolene	Attitudes	P	112
Lausch, Ed	Stitch Of Time	I	241
McKown, Michael	Weathering The Storm	I	26
Quick, Corlin	Our Castle	I	49
Quick, Marie	Little Mona Lisa	P	195

Rice, Denny	True Blue	C	233
Seidman, Laurence	Jackie	W	100
Voorhees, Rich	Striking	P	45
Wilson, Doran	Fuel Management	D/T	136
Wilson, Doran	Stamping Die	D/P	211
Wood, Nancy	1, 2, 3, Out	I	194
Wyant, James	The Mirror In Grandma's Attic	P	44

IOWA

Belling, Bruce	Free Spirit	P	113
Carney, James	Tears Of A Mountain	I	91
Donhauser, Rick	Book Sales	C	76
Fagan, Gary	Everything's Okay	W	153
Fischer, Suzanne C.	Scouting The Way	I	47
Fraise, Dennis	Vintage Collector	P	218
Grabill, Barbara	Little One's Bath	I	19
Kopecky, Susan	Primary Presentation	I	60
Ricks, Mary Anne	Serenity	I	228
Ricks, Mary Anne	True To His Nature	P	127
Scarff, Hope	The Phantom Artist	I	243

KANSAS

Blosser, Kelly	Balance And Grace	W	102
Brent, Philip D.	Our Love Story	A	249
Locklear, Jeff	Companionship	I	126
McDaniels, Kem	Yesterday's Bride	W	103
Perryman, John	Altamaha Swamp	I	109
Perryman, John	Autumn Splendor	I	187
Rees, Charlie	Evening Sail	I	53
Velia, Nema	Mac	NEG	185

KENTUCKY

Carter, Harry W.	Cascading Crystals	S	61
Carter, Harry W.	Eccentric Kaleidoscope	S	61
Fraley, Randy G.	Alone And Forgotten	P	38
Fraley, Sandy	Cherish The Child	P	73
Fraley, Sandy	The Lookout	I	166
Powell, Victoria Austin	Toot, Toot, Toot	P	194
Walden, Beverly	Captured Innocence	P	39
Walden, Beverly	Eye Of the Storm	P	25
Walden, Timothy	Fender Bender	P	150
Walden, Timothy	His Father's Eyes	P	25
Walden, Timothy	The Aristo-Crab	P	164
Walden, Timothy	Age Of Innocence	P	39
Yonts, Barbara	Come Play With Me	P	73
Yonts, Barbara	Whispers Of Love	W	33

LOUISIANA

Abshire, Donna	Timeless Elegance	W	56
Estes, Donna	Satin Roses & Silk Magnolias	W	34
Faust, Robert	Great Great Grandparents	D/RE	223
Hannan Jr., John Michael	Julianna And Jared's Love Story	A	248
LaCour, Michael	Crimson Sunset	I	171
O'Halloran, William	A Kiss To Build A Dream On	W	153
Tompkins, David	Romance In Saint Patrick's Cathedral	W	56
Voclain, Kirk	Sister, Sister	P	12
Weaver, Larry	A Time Remembered	I	30
Weaver, Larry	Peace In The Valley	I	159

MAINE

Boucher, Felice	Adam & Eve	I	190
Haskell, Mark	Hey What's He Looking At	I	85

MARYLAND

Campanellie, Joseph	Seaside Blues	P	20
Mohamed, Nizam	Love Makes The World Go Round	W	55

MASSACHUSETTS

Barnes, Richard	Dog-Gone-It	P	22
Damianos, Lynne	Dynawave Connectors	C	135
Damianos, Lynne	Sunflower Sunset	I	60
Foley, Jack	Dog Day Afternoon	I	131
Foley, Jack	The Watergirl	P	263
Henriques, Steven	Wrapped Up In Your Love	W	153
Meritt, Roger	A Reflection At Pemaquid	I	27
Skerry, Michael	Blue Heaven	W	16
Skerry, Michael	Winter Wonderland	W	33
Smith, Denise	Wash-A-Bye-Baby	I	263
Souza, John F.	Steppin Out	I	208
*Spencer, Mark	Roots	P	96
*Spencer, Mark	Wonderland	P	82
Ward, Karen	Generations	P	81
Zemba, Robert F.	Don't Let Go	I	263

MICHIGAN

Abel, Patrick	A Born Leader	P	9
Davison, Randy	Hey Mom Quick Look At Nick	P	23
Derocher, Joe	Solitude	P	164
Deutsch, David M.	A Moment Of Solitude	P	207
Deutsch, David M.	The Arrogance Of Youth	P	207
Dupras, Scott	Amanda	P	244
Dupras, Scott	Austin's Debut	P	20
Dupras, Scott	Diamond In The Rough	P	209
Dupras, Scott	Spell Bound	P	42
Frederick, James	Hidden	I	44
Galetto, Michael	A Silent Cry	P	116
Gleason, Rod	Gypsy Pride	P	129
Marion, John	Dream Quenchers	D/P	266
Murin, Helen	I Still Love You Grandma	P	194
Nelson, John	In Her Wildest Dreams	D/P	162
Nichols, Ronald	Enough To Share	P	186
Rankin, Barry	William's Way	P	243
Rankin, Barry	California Dreamer	P	10
Schmelzer, James	The Main Event	A	141
Stewart, Robert L.	Snake River Overlook	I	52
Wares, Karen	Only View Available	NEG	255
Yancy, Helen	After Millenniums	D/T	231
Yancy, Helen	Vortex Of Silence	D/T	61

MINNESOTA

Graupmann, John	Old World Charm	I	203
Lunderby, Ken	Second Hand Rose	P	195
Motzko, Linda	Enchanted Passage	I	166
Riddell, John	He's Mine All Mine	P	191
Saladin, Kay	Jacob — Red Striped Shirt	NEG	184
Saladin, Kay	Scar Face	NEG	255
Tamm, Roger	The Lord Is My Light	P	178
Wentink Jr., James T.	Eye See You	C	77

MISSISSIPPI

Stewart, Buddy M.	One Floor From Heaven	W	142
Stewart, Buddy M.	Rapunzel	P	242

MISSOURI

Bonsall, Janet	Follow Through	I	94
DeLaney, Jeffery	And They Prayed…	W	191
Harvey, Gerald	Five Of A Kind	I	93
Rockafellow, Chris John	Mr. Hyde Lurking In The Darkness	C	260
Swoboda, Dave	Dimensions	I	62
Tiefenbrunn, Cindy	Dave	NEG	185
Wilks, Rhonda	Here's Lookin' At You, Kid	I	40
Wright, Mark Allen	Technical Merit	C	77
Wright, Mark Allen	Yellow Roadster	C	174

MONTANA

McMillan, M.A.	Drummer	P	192
McMillan, M.A.	Snow Squall	I	130
Wierda, Kathy J.	Montana Gold	P	124
Winslow, Steven	Extended Elegance	C	190

NEBRASKA

Baer, Brian	Arms Of Aspiration	I	62
Baer, Brian	The Sky Is Not The Limit	I	52
Cunningham, Richard	Hoop Dreams	I	63
Frieze, James	Attitude	P	180
Hansen, Russell L.	The Game Of Life Don't Play It Alone	I	128
Hansen, Russell L.	Womanscycle	I	236
Moore, LC	Angles And Curves	I	243
Rader, Richard	Passage Through O'Hare	I	163
Reese, James	Gam Paw's Girl	P	75
Vance, Tina Marie	Childhood Treasures	P	99

NEW HAMPSHIRE

Walsh, Jane	Pause On A Misty Morning	I	124

NEW JERSEY

Chamberlain, Jim	Monet's Garden	D/P	204
Clipper, Neal H.	Two Hot Dogs, Hold The Mustard	W	54
Currens, John	Blue Thunder	C	174
Currens, John	Van Goghs Bouquet	C	251
Currens, John	XRay Shoe	C	217
Derex, David	The Producer David Brown	P	70
Gabelli, Gene	Manhatten Bridge	I	175
Kahn, Bob	Style And Grace	W	138
Kephart, Lorraine	Madisen	P	7
LaSala, Jim	Birth Of A Flower	I	59
Lista, Gene	Scarecrow	P	221
Maddaloni, Anthony P.	Golden Orifice	I	145
Maddaloni, Anthony P.	Morning Light North Rim	I	227
Maddaloni, Anthony P.	Thunderstorm Badlands, SD	I	29
Martins, Maria	My Bear	P	74
Martins, Marla	Wind Beneath My Wings	P	120
Molnar, John	My Daddy	W	140
Weinerman, Alan	Endless Threads	C	234
Weinerman, Alan	Mustang Heaven	C	261
Weinerman, Martha "Marty"	New York, New York	I	264

NEW MEXICO

Hohnstreiter, Glenn F.	Moment Of Glory	I	91
Lozoya, Oscar	Jugando Con La Muerte (Playing With Death)	I	156
Lozoya, Oscar	Mask	I	262
Lozoya, Oscar	Vidra	P	70
Lozoya, Oscar	Eyes Of Winter	P	157
Spitznagle, Alan	Faded Dreams	I	122

NEVADA

Palen, Stephen	Autumn Morn	I	28

NEW YORK

Bergano, Steven	Enchanted Moment	W	69
Bernstein, Paul	Brian's Bar Mitzvah	A	248
Cashmere, Art	Up In Arms	W	110
Dantoni, Robert	Irish Country Road	I	227
Drew, Colleen	A Moment Of Solitude	W	152
Fetzner, Karin B.	Story Teller	P	149
Fundalinski, Bogdan J.	The Awakening Of Spring	I	59
Green, Shirley E.	Grandma's Favorites	P	80
Guerrina, Lizbeth	My Prince My Camelot	P	8
Hesslink, Mindy	Hurry Home	I	63
Johnson, Janice	Rapid Action	I	127
Lloyd, Jacquelyn	Opposites Attract	I	226
Loria, Marlene	For The Cover	COLO	118
Loria, Marlene	Isabella	COLO	185
Mantler, Jeffrey H.	Portal Of Love	W	14
Marchisotto, Richard	Grandma's Pie	C	259
Marchisotto, Richard	Spicy Sauce	C	259
Muska, Debrah	A Breed Apart	P	254

The print entitled "In a Mellow Zone" from the 1997 Loan Collection was incorrectly credited. Photo credit belongs to Mark Spencer.

Muska, Debrah	Mo & Flo	P	254
Pfleiderer, Renate	Nouvelle Cuisine	C	259
Restrepo, Bernardo	Hey Guys Play A Song For Us	W	66
Restrepo, Bernardo	Our Love Lights The House Of God	W	142
Ruymen, Robert	Sun Of God	I	256
Ruymen, Robert	Your Day Will Come	W	103
Sauro, Duane	A Stroll In Time	D/P	95
Sauro, Duane	Boss Bikes And Barmaids	D/P	261
Sauro, Duane	Flowers In The Attic	D/P	245
Sauro, Duane	Statuesque	D/P	206
Schmitt, Brian	Hardworking Harvest	I	146
Schmitt, Brian	The Calm Before The Storm	I	121
Setchell, Pamela	Gentle Champions	P	254
Small, Jerry	A Kiss Before The Storm	W	68
Stevenson, William	The Choir Master	P	178
Upitis, Augusts	Morning Pearls	I	59

NORTH CAROLINA

Brogan-Bowen, Dot	Grandmother's Twins	D/RE	223
GoForth, Karen	The Last Supper	I	189
McNeilly, Mary	Embrace	P	193
McNeilly, Randy	Head Of The Class	D/T	179
Melvin, Ralph	When Two Become One	A	199
Metsker, Annell L.	Rhapsody In Blue	P	51
Weaver, Linda	Hannah	COLO	119
Weaver, Linda	Jacob	COLO	119
Weaver, Linda	Profile Of Poverty	P	157

NORTH DAKOTA

Hanson, Russ	Borrowed Bucks	C	137
Hanson, Russ	Light Fantasies	C	137
Hanson, Russ	The Grain Grows On	I	107
Nysetvold, Paul	Watchful Eye	COLO	84
Robideau, Jim	Window To The Past	I	158
Scherling, Larry	A Penny For Your Thoughts	P	72
Scherling, Larry	The Little White Cloud	I	31
Stegman, Scott	Gets The Red Out	NEG	184
Stegman, Scott	Turning The Other Cheek	NEG	184

OHIO

Ayers, Michael	All I Ask Of You	A	248
Ayers, Michael	Columbus Nightfall	I	264
Ayers, Michael	Nevada Neon	I	177
Bass, Richard A.	Hay Seed	P	83
Bohland, Mark A.	Fleeting Mist	I	252
Boylan, Doug	Shaped By Nature	I	262
Brown, Kevin	Cathedral Of Admiration	W	14
Carroll, Ron	Elegant Romance	W	57
Crumley, Polly	Curiosity	P	74
Finlay, Barry	Whirlpool Sculpture	C	161
Houdashelt, Randy	Wrapped In Her Thoughts	P	221
Huffman, Jerry	The Guitar Player	I	150
Hughes, Robert	A Walk In The Clouds	W	32
Hughes, Robert	The Loss	D/P	132
Hughes, Robert	Three Brothers	I	130
Hughes, Robert	A Reflection Of Love	W	32
Johnson, Jon	The First Snow	P	46
Johnson, Jon	Hi Tech In Blue	I	183
Johnson, Jon	Out Of The Blue	P	183
Kelly, Ross	Carolina Sunrise	P	11
Kotar, Ronald	The Grandeur Of Love	W	143
Kunesh, Robert	Genesis	W	111
Lavoie, Rex	Structural Geometrics	C	230
Miller, T. Paul	West Minster	C	250
Miller, T. Paul	Liquid Steel	C	233
Miller, T. Paul	Sunset Over Cinci	C	215
Moss, David	Showoff	I	239
Newell Jr., Richard	Alone	P	21

Owen, Matthew	From Fantasy To Reality	C	174
Owen, Matthew	Elegant Irons	C	210
Pfohl, Sandra	Older Than I Wanna Be	NEG	255
Prince, Paul	Child's Play	P	201
Ramseyer, Fredrick	Crystal Moment	C	232
Ramseyer, Fredrick	Honest Day's Work	P	149
Rapini, Kathi	Red Moon's Rising	I	219
Rice, Patrick	Swept Away	W	143
Scavnicky, Ladd	Gothic Passion	W	143
Smith, Bill	Furnace Fire Works	I	171
Sommers, Kathryn	Mad About You	P	116
Tilley, Ed	Kegg Pipe Organ Builder	C	250
Tobias, Beth	Sugar Everything Nice	P	224
Wagner, Theodore A.	Sailing Home	P	51
Weekley, Rachael	Innocence	P	80
Wolfe, Douglas	Fallen Angel	P	242

OKLAHOMA

Arnold, Dori	Pretty In Pink	P	38
Horton, Dwaine	Majestic Bride	W	35
Lobit Jr., Edgar	Dusty Serengetti Trails	I	158
Martin, Dennis	Garden Of The Gods	I	145
Martin, Mel	On The Move	I	123
Payne, Loy A.	The Golf Lesson	P	129
Scott, Mike	Profile Of Love	W	198

OREGON

Barry, Kevin	Follow Me	P	114
Fant, Michael	Avocet Elegance	P	58
Fant, Michael	Colorful Getaway	P	58
Kassab, Cindy	Sleepy Harbor	I	252
Kassab, Cindy	Sunflowers Everywhere	I	79
Klages, Walter	Warm Memories	P	240
Lamping, Lisa	Come And Get Me	P	180
Lamping, Lisa	Sands Of Time	P	50
Lapp-Murray, Linda	Welcome, Newborn	P	19
Lind, William	All Together Again	P	191
May, Richard	Imitation Of Solitude	P	165
Murray, Ian	Can't Catch Me	P	10
Murray, Ian	Dance Class	P	190
Roundy, Steve	Sundown Stop-Off	P	200
Rubens, Peter Paul	Ebb Tide	I	144
Sahagian, Sandy	Journey's End	I	236
Sahagian, Sandy	Where Land Meets The Sky	I	144

PENNSYLVANIA

Beitzel, Richard	And Then We Went Home	W	126
Davies, Linda	Weathered By Time	I	115
Good, Michael	Cittá Di Amoré	I	252
Heydorn, Pati	For A Kiss	W	23
Huddle Martin, Linda	The Long Way Home	P	80
Kimble, Christopher	Sharing A Moment	P	128
Long, Kenneth	Shades Of Passion	D/P	221
Miller, Martin	Little Wonders	P	82
Neubauer, Ferdinand	Beginning A Fairy Tale	W	48
Neubauer, Ferdinand	City Hideaway	P	48
Richards, Ron	I Believe I Can Fly	P	74
Richnavsky, John F.	Wedding Winds	W	35
Richnavsky, John F.	Ebony And Ivory	P	150
Rose, Jeffrey	Glenn Sullivan	W	66
Rose, Jeffrey	Love Leads The Way	W	142
Sherman, Cathy	That's Life	S	134
Shipman, John L.	The Magic Is In The Hands	P	193
Stewart, Joan E.	Sea Urchins	I	106
Stewart, Joan E.	Spike	P	225

RHODE ISLAND

Merritt Swart, Sally	A Mile In My Shoes	P	157

Thibeault, Gary — Foxwoods Resort Casino — C — 214
Thibeault, Gary — Grand Pequot Tower Lobby — C — 88

SOUTH CAROLINA

McMullin, Brad — Elegance — C — 233
Matuska, Edgar W. — I Am The Artistic Director — P — 148
Monahan, Tom — Touch Of Country — P — 242

SOUTH DAKOTA

Richter, Ralph O. — Waimea Canyon — I — 28

TENNESSEE

Andrews, Hud — Graphic Designer — P — 148
Dean, Larry — Out Of Time — D/T — 204
Jacobs, Jeffrey — Courtyard At Dawn — C — 215
Jacobs, Jeffrey — Promus - Call Center — C — 89
Jacobs, Jeffrey — St. Mary's Auditorium — C — 88
Oakley, Patty — Little Boy Blue — P — 117
Ullery, Curt — Pen And Pencil — C — 161
Wallace, Dustine — Diddy-up Towboy — P — 83
White, Barbara — Pretty Miss — P — 38

TEXAS

Baker, Sharon — Lucifer's Lure — I — 131
Balthazar, George N. — A Moment Of Solitude — W — 13
Binegar Jr., Jim — Summer Splendor — I — 121
Cricchio, Frank — You And Me Against The World — P — 68
Cruger, Elizabeth — Balance — P — 244
Davison, Darlyn — Awesome Eyes — P — 108
Hendrie, Vaughn — A Day With Great Grandpa — I — 186
Hezel, Till — Stir Fry — C — 77
Hezel, Till — Welcome To The Bates' Motel — I — 214
Hoermann, Susan — A Timeless Feeling — W — 13
Kincheloe, Lewis — Placa Rosa — P — 20
Kozak, Steve — Simple Pleasures — P — 45
Kreimborg, Deborah — God's Pasture — I — 30
McMullen, Gary — State-Of-The-Art — C — 135
Murphey, Lisa — Dress Rehearsal — P — 18
Murphey, Lisa — Midnight Rodeo — D/RE — 41
Murphey, Lisa — Sirene — D/RE — 41
Murphey, Lisa — Tiger Lily — D/RE — 41
Murray, John M. — Dance In The Wind — W — 32
Nogle, Gail — First Chair — P — 193
Nogle, Gail — Lavender Blue — P — 18
Smith, Scott — The Mentalist — P — 179
Staudt, Rick — Maybe Daddy Was Right — W — 101
Stevens, James — Veiled Tragedy — P — 45
Wells, Dennis — Radiant Day — W — 246

UTAH

Busath, Don — Wagon Train — I — 104
Busath, Drake — Chief Justice Richard Howe — P — 71
Duncan, William — Angel — W — 35
Hansen, Dale P. — Lost In Time — I — 172
Hansen, Dale P. — Yippi Yi Yeah — W — 33
Kent, Cameron — Enchanted Engagement — P — 170
Mackley, Steve — And She Wept — I — 120
Mackley, Steve — If Rain Drops Were Lemondrops — I — 97
Mackley, Steve — Perched On Peril — I — 85
Newman, Dave — Wisdom — P — 178
Weitzeil, Gary — Midnight Sun — I — 86

VERMONT

Beltrami, Chris — A July 4th Wedding — A — 199
Beltrami, Chris — Playing Hooky — I — 94
Beltrami, Patricia — The Final Turn Towards Home — I — 115
Beltrami, Patricia — Winter Storm — I — 31
Hayes, Barry — The Contenders — I — 156

Jenks, Robert — Sightless Motion — I — 120
Parker, Charles A. — Spring Ice — I — 123
Parker, Charles A. — Midnight Blue — C — 134
Parker, Charles A. — Seeds Of Opportunity — C — 238

VIRGINIA

Austin, Allen — 97 Bride — W — 100
Fish, Jake — The Hour Of The Wolf — P — 108
Fish, Jake — A Pledge Of Allegiance — P — 237
Harris Jr., Robert L. — Twilight; Comet Hale-Bopp — I — 29
Hayes III, James H. — Graced In Tradition — P — 102
Hayes III, James H. — Leslie And Steve — A — 249
Hayes III, James H. — The Bottom Line — C — 256
Isaacs, Mollie — Silent Swimmer — I — 229
Martin, Richard — Cyber Madness — I — 135
Nelms, Carla — Heirloom Innocence — P — 99
Piacesi, William — Comfort — I — 162
Piacesi, William — When Darkness Comes — I — 245
Ratcliff, David — Wild Onions — I — 217
Stagner, James R. — Serenity — I — 59
Tiller, Gayle Tewksbury — Wave Dancer — P — 98
Toves, Beverly — Repose — P — 125

WASHINGTON

Cianci, Donald — Together We… Can — P — 50
Hudson, Bruce — Are You Sure You Saw (A) Whale? — P — 155
McCanless, Greg — Treasured Moments — P — 189
Simmons, Peter — Timeless — W — 16
Weston, Matthew — Little Dripper — C — 257
Whitmire, Ken — Down Home — P — 81
Whitmire, Ken — My Golden Hour — P — 200

WEST VIRGINIA

Bell, Michael — Silent Sentry — I — 26
Lawson, James T. — Boats At Motif #1 — I — 228
Lorenzen, Jurgen — Study In Bronze And Glass — I — 256
McNemar, Joe — The Red Piece — I — 257

WISCONSIN

Ahrens, Steven — Emily — P — 99
Ahrens, Steven — Sisters — P — 208
Allyn, Jon — Composed — I — 262
Carlson, Chris — Innocence — P — 73
Carney, Sandra — Consoling — P — 220
Caylor, Carl — Intense Perspective — P — 181
Drake, Darton — Show Girl — P — 219
Duenkel, Fuzzy — Back Porch Blues — P — 245
Duenkel, Fuzzy — Guenevere — P — 96
Duenkel, Fuzzy — Haunted — I — 47
Erickson, Jon — Beautiful Elegance — W — 34
Erickson, Jon — Father And Son — P — 254
Evenson, Carrie — Beautiful Dreamer — P — 125
Evenson, Carrie — Sheer Beauty — P — 125
Evenson, Carrie — The Look Of Love — P — 42
Hoff, Deborah — Tri Power — C — 210
Krueger, Kent — Eyes Of Sadness — P — 225
Kunstman, Mark K. — Safeway Up And Around — C — 133
Larsen, Lee — Carrie — P — 195
Larsen, Lee — Oh My! — P — 74
Lom-Ourada, Trudy — The Deep Blue — COLO — 176
Luedtke, Lisa — Freedom — COLO — 84
Luedtke, Lisa — The Beauty Beyond — COLO — 205
Martin-Lemmen, Susan — Victorian Charm — COLO — 223
Meulemans, Angela — Dressed For The Holidays — COLO — 205
Meulemans, Angela — My Three Little Angels — COLO — 118
Schaefer Hees, Alexandra — Natural Phenomenon — I — 144
Schwartz, Dennis G. — Dairy-Aire — I — 240
Sohns, Michael — Appointment With Destiny — D/P — 172

Stoller, Daniel	Dad's Evening Excursion	I	146
Stoller, Daniel	Thee Gathering Place	C	163
Totushek, Mille	A Man Of Few Words	P	165
Wacker, David G.	Good Morning My Love	I	187
Wacker, David G.	The Golden Years	I	114
Wacker, Jean A.	Makes You Sneeze	D/P	231
Wacker, John D.	Good To the Last Drop	I	91
Weyenberg, Susan	Sidewalk Soloist	COLO	222
Zettler, Robert G.	Protective Custody	P	116

WYOMING

Carpenter, Richard	An October Moment	I	78
Mock, Robert	Floating Fantasy	I	169
Mudd, Lou	Desert Rose	I	124

INTERNATIONAL

CANADA
ALBERTA

Brouwer, Jr., Dirk	Sittin' Pretty	P	266
Wright, Douglas J.	Evening Crossing	I	105
Wright, Douglas J.	Wood Sculptor	P	180

BRITISH COLUMBIA

Montizambert, Dave	Lord Of The Violin	D/P	179

QUEBEC

Robillard, Julie	Immortality	P	154
Simone, Louise	Metamorphosis	P	43

MANITOBA

Ulicki, Andrew	Alpine Utopia	I	27
Ulicki, Andrew	Rainy Day Blues	P	116

ONTARIO

Baldini, Jacqueline	Misty Rose	I	79
Bell, Richard	BSA-3	C	160
Bell, Richard	Monetti Pens	C	161
Friesner, Shawn	Hot Pink Packard	I	260
Gagnon, Claude J.	Fascination	W	34
Jacob, Hugh R.	Reflections Of Life	P	11
Rudd, Stephen	Vertical Elegance	P	208

COSTA RICA

Rojas, Armando	Communion	P	209

DENMARK

Reedorf, Kitty	For Better Or Worse	W	65
Reedorf, Kitty	The Color Of Love	P	139

ENGLAND

Dyer, Pamela Anne	Reflective Sunrise	I	145
Dyer, Peter	Long Wait Over	W	101
Green, Charles	Kingsley's List	P	181
Kaye, Su	Flight Path	I	202
Kaye, Su	Step Out Of The Window	I	218

INDONESIA

Iskandar, Jemmy	Victorian Bride	W	64
Leonardi, Indra	Classique Beauty	W	139
Leonardi, Indra	Melody Of Love	W	138
Leonardi, Indra	Shanghai Bride	W	139
Paulus, Djoni	Always Close To You	W	65
Piauw Tjong, Tjhang	Sensuality	W	64
Piauw Tjong, Tjhang	Sleeping Beauty	W	64
Sioe, Steven Ing Ming	Crystal Ball Chain	C	234

IRELAND

Travers, James	End Of A Perfect Day	W	56

JAPAN

Hasegawa, Masayuki	My Memorial Day	W	197
Hayashi, Kiyomi	Bright Autumn All Weather	P	95
Hayashi, Yoshinori	Let's Start To Bright Future	P	14
Hayashi, Yuki	Look For The Autumn	P	114
Kajiyama, Yasutaka	Quiet	P	197
Koshino, Norihisa	Water Fall With A Bride	P	198
Koshino, Norihisa	White Wedding Cup	P	198

KOREA

Kim, Hun	An Aroma Of Roses	P	246

MEXICO

Castelan, Abel	Tears Of Life	I	237
Castelan, Genaro	The Plough Man	I	105
Castelan, Genaro	The Survivors	I	168
Castelan, Genaro	Violent Eruptions	I	147
Perez, Basilio Perez	La Historia Del Uino	P	218

NORWAY

Larsen, IB	Scandinavian Winter	P	46

PERU

Farah, Monica			
	Perika's Stuff Transforms Wicker Into A Piece Of Art	C	204

PUERTO RICO

Alvarez, Jose	Brenda	P	207
Alvarez, Jose	Daniel	P	151
Alvarez, Jose	Ramon	P	148
Aragon, Juan	Unseen Blossom	I	79
Aragon, Juan	Yellowish	I	253
Toro, Max	My Favorite Spot	C	213

SOUTH WALES

Ellis, Peter	The Love I Lost	W	166

SPAIN

Limeres, Tony	From Past To Future	W	37

VIDEO ENTRIES

LOCATION /NAME	TITLE	CATEGORY
CALIFORNIA		
Goolsby, John	Off Duty Shooting	V/CCI
Goolsby, John	Sandy Spin Slade	V/CCI
Goolsby, John	Nestle Teams In Action	V/CCI
Goolsby, John	The Hudson Wedding	V/SE
FLORIDA		
Keelan, Kevin L.	A Western Dream	V/SE
Keelan, Kevin L.	A Golden Memory	V/SE
Keelan, Kevin L.	Looking Back Looking Ahead	V/SE
Keelan, Kevin L.	Family Affair	V/SE
MARYLAND		
Dalcin, Richard	Players Family Amusement C.	V/CCI
Dalcin, Richard	Baltimore Co. Firefighters Assoc.	V/CCI
Dalcin, Richard	Laser Applications Inc.	V/CCI
Dalcin, Richard	MD Professional Photo Assoc.	V/CCI
NEBRASKA		
Binder, Kevin	Tuffshell Tanks	V/CCI
Binder, Kevin	Wedding Video Demo	V/SE
Binder, Kevin	Composite Drill Pipe	V/CCI
NEW JERSEY		
Brockmann, Clifford	Bagel Divider And Former	V/CCI
Brockmann, Clifford	Helping Families Stay Together	V/CCI
Brockmann, Clifford	Era TV	V/CCI
Brockmann, Clifford	PNM Plus	V/CCI
Gellman, Gary	Boys Will Be Boys	V/CCI
Gellman, Gary	Our Son's Day	V/SE
Gellman, Gary	How Beautiful	V/SE
Gellman, Gary	Bad To The Bone	V/SE
Lista, Gene	Wedding Promo Dave & Andrea	V/SE
Lista, Gene	NJ Convention Music Tribute	V/SE
NEW YORK		
Stevens, Bart	W. Highlights John & Ann	V/SE
Stevens, Bart	W. Highlights Chris & Lisa	V/SE
Stevens, Bart	Training Tape Colorado/Prime	V/CCI
Stevens, Bart	Our Love Story Ron & Rosemary	V/SE

LOCATION /NAME	TITLE	CATEGORY
NORTH CAROLINA		
Strowd, Charles	Glow Of Orange In The Cold	V/CCI
Strowd, Charles	Carolina Sketches — House In the Horseshoe	V/CCI
OHIO		
Wurzell, John	Prof. Photo Oh.	V/CCI
Wurzell, John	Creative Video Flying Logo	V/CCI
Wurzell, John	Enhance Your Image	V/CCI
Wurzell, John	The Video Zone	V/CCI
TENNESSEE		
Carrier III, William	Titanic The Exhibition	V/CCI
Carrier III, William	The Freedom Awards	V/CCI
Carrier III, William	Partners In Public Education	V/CCI
Carrier III, William	No Deals	V/CCI
TEXAS		
Rash, Mark	Quality Healthcare	V/CCI
Rash, Mark	Moments Like These	V/CCI
Rash, Mark	Location Location Location	V/CCI
Rash, Mark	Banking Comfort	V/CCI
Payton, Steve	MTS #1 In The Nation	V/CCI
Payton, Steve	The Games Of Texas	V/CCI
Payton, Steve	Season's Greetings '97	V/SE
Payton, Steve	From Field To Finished Bale	V/CCI

COMPETITION JUDGES

1998 JURY CHAIRS
Jim Frieze, M.Photog., Cr.
Robert Golding, M.Photog., Cr., PPA Certified, Hon.M.Photog.
Colbert Howell, M.Photog., Cr., PPA Certified, Hon.M.Photog.
Roland Laramie, M.Photog., Cr., PPA Certified, A-ASP. Hon.M.Photog.
Duncan MacNab, M.Photog., Cr., PPA Certified
Tim Mathiesen, M.Photog., Cr., A-ASP, F-ASP*
Warren Motts, M.Photog., Cr., PPA Certified, Hon.M.Photog, A-ASP, Hon.A-ASP
Marvel Nelson, M.Photog., Cr., Hon.M.Photog., F-ASP, Hon.F-ASP, Hon A-ASP
Robert M.Opfer, M.Photog., Cr., Hon.M.Photog., PPA Certified
Barry Rankin, M.Photog., Cr.
Paul Schultz, M.Photog., Cr.
William F. Stevenson, M.Photog., Cr.
Michael Taylor, M.Photog., Cr., F-ASP*
Bill S. Weeks, M.Photog., Cr., PPA Certified, A-ASP
Helen Yancy, M.Photog., M.Artist., MEI.,Cr., Hon.M.Photog., PPA Certified, A-ASP*

PORTRAIT/WEDDING
Gabriel Alonso, M.Photog., Cr., PPA Certified
Hud Andrews, M.Photog., Cr., PPA Certified*
Pat Beltrami, M.Photog., Cr.
Rod Brown, M.Photog., Cr.
Bill Bruton, M.Photog., Cr., PPA Certified
Jerry Costanzo, M.Photog., Cr., PPA Certified
Dennis Craft, M.Photog., Cr., PPA Certified
Len Dixon, M.Photog., Cr.
Peter Dyer, M.Photog., Cr., F-ASP
Don Emmerich, M.Photog., MEI.,Cr.*
Kaye Frey, M.Photog., M.Artist,Cr., PPA Certified*
Patty Geist, M.Photog., Cr.
Robert Glover
Charles Green, M.Photog., MEI.,Cr.
Jack Holowitz, M.Photog., Cr.
David Huntsman, M.Photog., Cr., PPA Certified*
Ed Matuska, M.Photog., Cr., A-ASP
Peggy McAteer, M.Photog., Cr., PPA Certified
J. Michael McBride, M.Photog., Cr.
Gary Meek, M.Photog., Cr., PPA Certified
Ron Nichols, M.Photog., Cr.
Ralph Pyle, M.Photog., Cr., PPA Certified
Richard Rader, M.Photog., Cr., PPA Certified
Terry Reinbold, M.Photog., Cr.
David Smith, M.Photog., Cr., F-ASP
Ron Stewart, M.Photog., Cr., PPA Certified
Richard Turner, M.Photog., Cr.*

COMMERCIAL
Hud Andrews, M.Photog., Cr., PPA Certified*
Stephen Best, M.Photog., Cr.
Bill Bruton, M.Photog., Cr., PPA Certified
William Carrier, III, M.Photog.MEI.,Cr., PPA Certified
Don Emmerich, M.Photog.MEI.,Cr.*
Dave Huntsman, M.Photog., Cr., PPA Certified*
Dominic Iodice, M.Photog.MEI.,Cr., PPA Certified
Sam Oliver, M.Photog., Cr.
Wayne Thom, M.Photog., Cr., F-ASP
Richard Turner, M.Photog., Cr.*
Richard Vorhees, M.Photog., Cr., PPA Certified
Doran Wilson, M.Photog.MEI.,Cr., PPA Certified

ELECTRONIC IMAGING
Bill Bruton, M.Photog., Cr., PPA Certified
William Carrier, III, M.Photog.MEI.,Cr., PPA Certified
Don Emmerich, M.Photog.MEI.,Cr.
Dominic Iodice, M.Photog.MEI.,Cr., CEI, PPA Certified
Ron Nichols, M.Photog., Cr.
Richard Rader, M.Photog., Cr., PPA Certified
Charles Strowd, MEI.,Cr.CEI
Richard Turner, M.Photog., Cr.*
Nema Velia, M.Artist., Cr.
Doran Wilson. M.Photog.MEI.,Cr., PPA Certified

ART/TECH
Gail Degnan, M.Artist., Cr., PPA Certified
Kaye Frey, M.Photog., M.Artist, Cr., PPA Certified*
Nancy Nicholson, M.Photog., Cr.
Nema Velia, M.Artist., Cr.
Linda Weaver, M.Photog., M.Artist., Cr., PPA Certified, F-ASP

JURY CHAIRS IN TRAINING
Hud Andrews, M.Photog., Cr., PPA Certified*
Dennis Craft, M.Photog., Cr., PPA Certified, F-ASP*
Peter Dyer, M.Photog., Cr., F-ASP
Dominic Iodice, M.Photog.MEI.,Cr., PPA Certified*
Richard Turner. M.Photog., Cr.*

OFFICIALS
Richard Vorhees, M.Photog., Cr., PPA Certified
Linda Weaver, M.Photog.,M.Artist., Cr., PPA Certified, F-ASP

*Members of the PEC Committee